Japanese
phrasebook

Kam Y Lau

Japanese Phrasebook
2nd edition

Published by
Lonely Planet Publications
Head Office: PO Box 617, Hawthorn, Vic 3122, Australia
Branches: 155 Filbert Street, Suite 251, Oakland CA 94607, USA
10 Barley Mow Passage, Chiswick, London W4 4PH, UK
71 bis rue de Cardinal Lemoine, 75005 Paris, France

Printed by
Colorcraft Ltd, Hong Kong

Cover photograph
Traditional calling cards (Chris Taylor)

Published
November 1994

This Book
This edition was written by Kam Y Lau. James Jenkin edited the book and
Sally Steward and Katie Purvis assisted in proofreading. Tamsin Wilson
was responsible for design, and Jane Hart designed the cover. Illustrations
were by Tamsin Wilson, Ann Jeffree, Margaret Jung and Angus Williams.
The Japanese script was provided by Kam Lau, and David Kemp and
Andrew Smith assisted with the script layout. For their assistance and
support, the author would like to thank his family, especially his daughter,
Sally. Thanks also to Hiroko Watanabe and Hitomi Ampo for their
invaluable advice. The author of the first edition was Kevin Chambers.

National Library of Australia Cataloguing in Publication Data

Lau, Kam Y
Japanese Phrasebook.
ISBN 0 86442 230 X.

1. Japanese language - Conversation and phrase books - English.
I. Title. (Series : Lonely Planet language survival kit).

495.683421

Contents

Introduction

Japanese pronunciation presents few problems for an English speaker, and expressing simple ideas in speech is straightforward. In addition, the standard language is spoken by Japan's 125 million inhabitants with little regional variation. Therefore you'll find it easy to communicate as you travel around Japan.

There is no proven direct link between Japanese and any other language. However, it has strong structural similarities to Korean, and bears some resemblance to Altaic languages such as Mongolian and Turkish. Although Japanese is grammatically unrelated to Chinese, over 1500 years ago Japan adopted the Chinese writing system, which uses ideographic characters (ie symbols which represent ideas rather than sounds). However, the written languages have grown apart, in particular because the Japanese later devised two syllabic alphabets which they use in combination with Chinese characters: *katakana*, said to have been invented by Kibi No Makibi (693-755), for the representation of foreign words and names; and *hiragana*, probably invented by the monk Kukai (774-835), for Japanese grammatical endings and some native words.

After a period of complete isolation, Japan began to open up in the mid-19th century, adopting many aspects of Western culture, administration and technology. As part of this process which has continued to the present day, Japanese has borrowed thousands of foreign words, in particular from English, such as *terebi*, 'TV' and *zūmu renzu*, 'zoom lens'. Often a native word and a borrowed word coexist – for example, 'milk' can be called either *gyūnyū* or *miruku*. Borrowed words are more commonly

7

used in the cities, and are quite fashionable among younger people. However, some older Japanese look down on these imported words, and a person in the country may not know what you're talking about! For this reason, two alternatives are sometimes given in this book.

Have a great trip – *yoi go-ryokō o!*

Seal said to be awarded from Chinese Han Emperor to the Japanese Emperor 57 AD – actual size

Pronunciation

Japanese pronunciation offers few difficulties for English speakers. It has no tones, unlike other languages in the region, and many of its sounds are found in English. The few things to watch are explained below.

Vowels

a	as the 'u' in 'cup'
e	as the 'e' in 'get'
i	as the 'i' in 'bit'
o	as the 'o' in 'lot'
u	as the 'u' in 'put'

Long Vowels
When a vowel is doubled, or written with a line above it, it must be pronounced twice as long as a short vowel. This is important as vowel length can change the meaning of a word: *yuki* means 'snow', while *yūki* means 'bravery'.

Reduced Vowels
The vowel **u** is sometimes not pronounced. The most common instances are:
• between **k** and **s** (eg *gakusei*, 'student', sounds like *gaksei*);

• in the verb endings *-desu* and *-masu* (eg *ii desu*, 'It's good', sounds like *ii des*).

Consonants

Most consonant sounds are similar to English, with the following important exceptions:
• **r** is made with a single flap of the tip of the tongue against the ridge behind your front teeth, like a cross between English 'r' and 'l'.
• **h** before **u** sounds like an English 'f'.

Double Consonants

There is a slight pause between double consonants, as in the English 'part-time': *gakkō*, 'school', is pronounced *ga*(pause)*kō*.

Reading Japanese

Remember, if you do have trouble communicating, you can always point to the phrase in this book. Sometimes two or more Japanese words sound the same (for example, *kaki* can mean 'oyster' or 'persimmon'), but showing someone the characters will clear up any confusion.

Japanese is usually written vertically and from right to left. However, occasionally it is written horizontally, like English, especially in conjunction with numbers, Romanised Japanese, or English (as in this book).

Written Japanese is actually a combination of three different scripts. One of these consists of ideographic characters. The other two, *hiragana* and *katakana*, represent sounds.

Ideographic Characters
Ideographic characters represent meanings rather than sounds. They may be made up of anything from one to over 20 strokes.

Chinese Characters – *kanji* Over the centuries, Japanese has borrowed thousands of words from Chinese, along with the system the Chinese used to write them. Over two thousand of these characters are still in everyday use. Furthermore, Japanese often combine *kanji* to create an unlimited number of new words.

Japanese Characters – *kokuji* The Japanese have supplemented *kanji* with several hundred of their own ideographic characters.

Phonetic Characters
Japanese also has two 'phonetic' scripts – that is, each character represents a sound or a combination of sounds.

Hiragana Adopted in order to represent particles and grammatical endings peculiar to Japanese, these characters are placed alongside the ideographic characters. Therefore, a single Japanese word may contain both scripts.

Katakana It's worth becoming familiar with these characters, as they are used to indicate the many recent borrowings from other languages.

PRONUNCIATION

HIRAGANA

あ a	い i	う u	え e	お o
か ka	き ki	く ku	け ke	こ ko
さ sa	し shi	す su	せ se	そ so
た ta	ち chi	つ tsu	て te	と to
な na	に ni	ぬ nu	ね ne	の no
は ha	ひ hi	ふ fu	へ he	ほ ho
ま ma	み mi	む mu	め me	も mo
や ya		ゆ yu		よ yo
ら ra	り ri	る ru	れ re	ろ ro
わ wa				を o
ん n				

きゃ kya	きゅ kyu	きょ kyo
しゃ sha	しゅ shu	しょ sho
ちゃ cha	ちゅ chu	ちょ cho
にゃ nya	にゅ nyu	にょ nyo
ひゃ hya	ひゅ hyu	ひょ hyo
みゃ mya	みゅ myu	みょ myo

りゃ rya	りゅ ryu	りょ ryo

が ga	ぎ gi	ぐ gu	げ ge	ご go
ざ za	じ ji	ず zu	ぜ ze	ぞ zo
だ da	ぢ ji	づ zu	で de	ど do

ぎゃ gya	ぎゅ gyu	ぎょ gyo
じゃ ja	じゅ ju	じょ jo

ば ba	び bi	ぶ bu	べ be	ぼ bo
ぱ pa	ぴ pi	ぷ pu	ぺ pe	ぽ po

びゃ bya	びゅ byu	びょ byo
ぴゃ pya	ぴゅ pyu	ぴょ pyo

KATAKANA

ア a	イ i	ウ u	エ e	オ o
カ ka	キ ki	ク ku	ケ ke	コ ko
サ sa	シ shi	ス su	セ se	ソ so
タ ta	チ chi	ツ tsu	テ te	ト to
ナ na	ニ ni	ヌ nu	ネ ne	ノ no
ハ ha	ヒ hi	フ fu	ヘ he	ホ ho
マ ma	ミ mi	ム mu	メ me	モ mo
ヤ ya		ユ yu		ヨ yo
ラ ra	リ ri	ル ru	レ re	ロ ro
ワ wa				ヲ o
ン n				

キャ kya	キュ kyu	キョ kyo
シャ sha	シュ shu	ショ sho
チャ cha	チュ chu	チョ cho
ニャ nya	ニュ nyu	ニョ nyo
ヒャ hya	ヒュ hyu	ヒョ hyo
ミャ mya	ミュ myu	ミョ myo

リャ rya	リュ ryu	リョ ryo

ガ ga	ギ gi	グ gu	ゲ ge	ゴ go
ザ za	ジ ji	ズ zu	ゼ ze	ゾ zo
ダ da	ヂ ji	ヅ zu	デ de	ド do

ギャ gya	ギュ gyu	ギョ gyo
ジャ ja	ジュ ju	ジョ jo

バ ba	ビ bi	ブ bu	ベ be	ボ bo
パ pe	ピ pi	プ pu	ペ pe	ポ po

ビャ bya	ビュ byu	ビョ byo
ピャ pya	ピュ pyu	ピョ pyo

Grammar

Knowing how to put a simple sentence together in Japanese will make communication even easier.

The Japanese choose particular words, and even change the forms of words, in order to show different levels of respect. This phrasebook generally uses the 'polite' style, which is suitable for most situations you will encounter.

As your aim is to speak Japanese, this chapter does not cover the very different conventions and rules of the written language.

Word Order
Unlike in English, where the word order is subject-verb-object, the order of a Japanese sentence is subject-object-verb. So, instead of saying 'I bought this phrasebook', a Japanese person will say the equivalent of 'I this phrasebook bought'. In addition, Japanese often omit the subject of a sentence if it is obvious or unimportant, leaving a sentence like 'This phrasebook bought' ('I' being obvious from the context). It means fewer words for you to worry about!

Articles
Japanese does not have words equivalent to 'a' and 'the'. For example:

It's **a** (or **the**) book.   *hon desu*
book is

14

However, if you want to point out a specific item, you can use words such as *kono* (this) and *sono* (that): *sono hon* 'the (that) book'.

Particles

A Japanese noun or pronoun is almost always followed by a 'particle'. These small but important words sometimes show us whether the preceding word is the subject or object of the sentence; at other times they are equivalent to English prepositions such as 'in' or 'to'.

wa

wa introduces the central topic of a sentence. The rest of the sentence then says more about this topic:

Mr Tanaka went.	*Tanaka san wa iki-mashita*
	Tanaka Mr *wa* went

ga & o

The particle *ga* marks the subject (who is doing something); while *o* marks the object (the person or thing that is having something done to it):

I bought the ticket.	*watashi ga kippu o kai-mashita*
	I *ga* ticket *o* bought

no

The particle *no* shows that something belongs to someone, a bit like '-'s' in English:

Mr Tanaka's car	*Tanaka san no kuruma*
	Tanaka Mr *no* car
my book	*watashi no hon*
	me *no* book

ni

The particle *ni* expresses:

• on what day or at what time:

on Tuesday	*kayōbi ni*
	Tuesday *ni*
at 3 o'clock	*san-ji ni*
	3 o'clock *ni*

• where something is:

at home	*uchi ni*
	home *ni*
in Japan	*nihon ni*
	Japan *ni*

• where you are going (destination):

| (I'm) going to Japan. | *nihon ni iki-masu* |
| | Japan *ni* go |

• why you are going somewhere:

| (I'm) going 'for shopping'. | *kai-mono ni iki-masu* |
| | shopping *ni* go |

de

The particle *de* indicates:

• the place of an action:

| I bought this at the department store. | *kore o depāto de kai-mashita* |
| | this *o* department store *de* bought |

• how someone or something gets somewhere:

I'm going by train.	*densha de iki-masu*
	train *de* go
I'll send it by airmail.	*kōkū bin de okuri-masu*
	airmail *de* send

• in what language:

| Please write in English. | *ei-go de kaite kudasai* |
| | English *de* write please |

e

The particle *e* indicates direction towards:

towards Tokyo	*Tōkyō e*
	Tokyo *e*
turn right	*migi e magari-masu*
	right *e* turn

Nouns

Compared to many languages, Japanese nouns are easy! They have no grammatical gender, or plural forms, so *gakusei* can mean 'student' or 'students':

GRAMMAR

I am a student.	*watashi wa gakusei desu*
	I *wa* student be
We are students.	*watashi tachi wa gakusei desu*
	we *wa* student be

Pronouns

Remember that a subject pronoun is often omitted when the person is obvious from the context.

GRAMMAR

I/me	*watashi*	we/us	*watashi tachi*
you (sing)	*anata*	you (pl)	*anata gata*
he/him	*kare*	they(m)	*kare ra*
she/her	*kanojo*	they (f)	*kanojo tachi*

Japanese uses particles and word order to distinguish between 'I' and 'me', 'she' and 'her' etc:

I'll call the doctor.	*watashi wa isha o yobi-masu*
The doctor will call me.	*isha wa watashi o yobi-masu*

You will also frequently hear other pronouns. In casual speech, men use *boku* for 'I/me', *wareware* for 'we/us', and *kimi* and *o-mae* for 'you'; and women use *atashi* for 'I/me', and *anta* for 'you'.

In very formal situations, Japanese use *watakushi* for 'I'.

This & That/Here & There

While English can only distinguish 'near the speaker' (this/here) and 'far from the speaker' (that/there), Japanese has three degrees of distance. The prefix *ko-* refers to something or someone close to the speaker; *so-* refers to something close to the listener; and *a-* refers to something far from both the speaker and the listener.

	near the speaker	near the listener	far from both
here/there/over there	*koko*	*soko*	*asoko*
this way/that way/ that way over there	*kochira*	*sochira*	*achira*
this/that/that over there	*kono* or *kore*	*sono* *sore*	*ano* *are*

GRAMMAR

The words *kono/sono/ano* come before a noun:

That train goes to Tokyo. *sono densha wa Tōkyō ni iki-masu*

While *kore/sore/are* stand on their own:

That is good. *sore wa ii desu*

Verbs

In some respects, Japanese verbs are simpler than English verbs. They do not change according to the subject: for example, *kai-masu* can mean 'I buy', 'you buy', 'he/she buys', 'we buy' and 'they buy'. In addition, Japanese has only two basic tenses: present and past, with the present being used to express the future.

Present Tense

If you look up a verb in a dictionary, you will usually find the Japanese *plain* form, which is not suitable for the polite style you should use. Unfortunately, it is difficult to work out the polite form from the plain form. For this reason, all the verbs in the vocabulary at the end of this book are given in the polite form, which ends in *-masu*.

I eat/you eat/he, she eats/we eat/they eat	tabe-**masu**

Remember that the verb usually goes at the end of the sentence.

I eat raw fish.	sashimi o tabe-masu raw fish o eat

To make a verb negative, replace the ending *-masu* with *-masen*:

I don't eat raw fish.	sashimi o tabe-**masen** raw fish o don't eat

Future Tense

Japanese has no future tense equivalent to English; use the present instead. To make it clear that you are talking about the future, you can use an appropriate time word such as *ashita* ('tomorrow'):

I'll go to Tokyo tomorrow.	ashita Tōkyō ni iki-**masu** tomorrow Tokyo ni go

Past Tense

To form the past tense, replace the polite ending *-masu* with *-mashita*:

I went to Tokyo. *Tōkyō ni iki-**mashita***

And to make the past tense negative, replace *-masu* with *-masen deshita*:

I didn't go to Tokyo. *Tōkyō ni iki-**masen deshita***

To Be

As in English, in Japanese the verb 'to be' is different from most other verbs. It has very peculiar negative forms! However, like other verbs, the endings do not change according to the subject: *desu* can mean 'I am', 'you are', 'he/she is', 'we are' and 'they are'.

Present	Present Negative	Past	Past Negative
am/are/is	am not/ aren't/isn't	was/were	wasn't/weren't
desu	*dewa arimasen*	*deshita*	*dewa arimasen deshita*

This isn't my bag. *kore wa watashi no kaban dewa arimasen*
this *wa* me *no* bag isn't

GRAMMAR

Requests

To ask for an item, simply name it and add *o kudasai*, meaning 'Please give me ...':

Please give me water.　　*mizu o kudasai*

To ask someone to do something, you use what is called the *-te* form of the verb, plus *kudasai*:

Please stop (the car).　　*tomete kudasai*

Unfortunately, the *-te* forms of verbs are just something you're going to have to learn. Here is a list of the *-te* forms of some useful verbs. Note that despite the name, they sometimes end in *-de*!

	polite form	**-te form**
buy	*kai-masu*	*katte*
call	*yobi-masu*	*yonde*
come	*ki-masu*	*kite*
eat	*tabe-masu*	*tabete*
go	*iki-masu*	*itte*
help	*tasuke-masu*	*tasukete*
hurry	*hayaku iki-masu*	*hayaku itte*
stop	*tomari-masu*	*tomatte*
wait	*machi-masu*	*matte*
write	*kaki-masu*	*kaite*

Adjectives

Japanese adjectives can come before nouns, just like in English:

expensive	*taka-i*
an expensive ticket	*taka-i kippu*

However, to say something **is** (expensive/beautiful/good etc) you have to distinguish between two types: *-i* adjectives and *na* adjectives. It is helpful to think of an *-i* adjective as a verb with its own special set of tense endings:

Present	Present Negative	Past	Past Negative
is expensive	isn't expensive	was expensive	wasn't expensive
*taka-**i desu***	*taka-**ku nai***	*taka-**katta***	*taka-**ku nakatta***

The ticket wasn't expensive.	*kippu wa taka-ku nakatta*

However, adjectives in *na* simply drop the *na* and combine with normal forms of 'to be':

pretty (flower)	*kirei na (hana)*
It's pretty.	*kirei desu*
It wasn't pretty.	*kirei dewa arimasen*

Adverbs

Many adverbs exist as words in their own right (eg *ashita*, 'tomorrow') and you can also change an *-i* adjective into an adverb by replacing the *-i* with *-ku*:

quick	*haya-i*
(She) walks quickly.	*haya-**ku** aruki-masu*

Questions

• To ask a yes/no question, just add *ka?* to the end of the sentence. Your voice also rises:

This is a book.	*kore wa hon desu*
Is this a book?	*kore wa hon desu ka?*
(I'm) going.	*iki-masu*
(Are you) going?	*iki-masu ka?*

• To find out specific information, you can use the Japanese equivalents of 'where', 'when', 'who' etc:

How?	*dō desu ka?*
How many?	*ikutsu desu ka?*
How much?	*ikura desu ka?*
What?	*nan desu ka?*
When?	*itsu desu ka?*
Where?	*doko desu ka?*
Who?	*donata desu ka?*

You can put these at the end of the sentence, for example:

Where is the library?	*toshokan wa doko desu ka?*
What is that?	*sore wa nan desu ka?*

• When a question involves a choice between two or more things, instead of using the word *mata wa* 'or', Japanese often repeat the question:

Are you an American
or an Australian?

*anata wa amerika-jin desu ka,
ōsutoraria-jin desu ka?*

Yes & No

Yes.	*hai* or *ee*
Certainly.	*hai, kashikomari mashita*
Yes it's true.	*hai, sō desu*
No.	*iie* or *iya*

A very polite way of asking a question is to use the negative form of the verb; so people may ask you a question like: *iki-masen ka?* 'Won't you go (with me)?'. If you answer *iie* 'no', it means, 'No, you are wrong, I **will** go'! To avoid confusion, instead of only answering with 'yes' or 'no', you can say the entire verb, for example:

(Yes,) I will go.	*iki-masu*
(No,) I won't go.	*iki-masen*

Modal Words
Must
To say someone 'must' or 'has to' do something, Japanese use the words *nakereba nari-masen* after a special form of the verb (as in the examples). However, if you use a different form it will still be understood.

(You) have to pay.	*harawa nakereba nari-masen*
(We) must wait.	*mata nakereba*
	nari-masen

To say that someone must **not** do something, add the words *wa ike-masen* to the *-te* form of the verb:

| Smoking is | *tabako o sutte wa ike-masen* |
| prohibited. | |

You can find more *-te* forms earlier under 'Requests'.

Want
Japanese has several ways of expressing 'want'.
• To say you want a particular item, say the thing then ... *ga hoshii desu*:

coffee	*kōhī*
I'd like a coffee.	*kōhī ga hoshii desu*
What would you like?	*nani ga hoshii*
	desu ka?

• To say that you want to do something, change the *-masu* ending on the verb to *-tai desu*:

| eat | *tabe-masu* |
| (I) want to eat. | *(watashi wa) tabe-tai desu* |

• To say that you **don't** want to do something, change the *-masu* ending on the verb to *-taku-nai desu*:

(I) don't want to eat.   *(watashi wa)*
                                 tabe-taku-nai desu

Allowed To

To ask if you are allowed to do something, add the words *mo ii desu ka?* to the *-te* form of the verb:

Can I take a photo?   *shashin o totte*
                           mo ii desu ka?
Can we come in?   *haitte mo ii desu ka?*

You can find more *-te* forms earlier under 'Requests'.

Ability in a Language

To say you 'can' or 'cannot' speak a language, say the name of the language plus *ga deki-masu* or *wa deki-masen*:

Can you speak English?   *ei-go ga deki-masu ka?*
I cannot speak   *nihon-go wa deki-masen*
Japanese.
I can speak a little   *nihon-go ga sukoshi dekimasu*
Japanese.

Some Useful Words
Place Words

above	... *no ue ni*	...の上に
behind	... *no ushiro ni*	...の後ろに
beside	... *no soba ni*	...のそばに
in front of	... *no mae ni*	...の前に

GRAMMAR

inside	... *no naka ni*	...の中に
left (of)	*(... no) hidari ni*	(...の)左に
next to	... *no tonari ni*	...の隣に
on top of	...*no ue ni*	...の上に
opposite	... *no mukai ni*	...の向かいに
	or ... *no mukō ni*	...の向こうに
outside	... *no soto ni*	...の外に
right (of)	*(... no) migi ni*	(...の)右に
under	... *no shita ni*	...の下に

Other Words

after	... *no ato*	...の後
always	*itsumo*	いつも
... and ...	... *to* ...	...と...
(in a list)	... *ya* ...	...や...
at	... *ni*	...に
in	... *ni*	...に
because	... *kara* ...	...から ...
	or ... *node* ...	...ので...
because of	... *no tame ni*	...の為に
before	... *no mae*	...の前
but	*shikashi*	しかし
forever	*itsu made mo*	いつまでも
from	... *kara*	...から
	or ... *yori*	...より
if (available)	*moshi (are)-ba*	若し(あれ)ば
(the) nearest	*moyori no* ...	最寄りの...
(be) necessary	*hitsu yō*	必要
now	*ima*	今
on (Sunday)	*(nichiyōbi) ni*	(日曜日)に
... or ...	... *mata wa* ...	...又は...

to	... *made*	...まで
towards	... *e*	...へ
together with	... *to issho ni*	...と一緒に
(me) too	*(watashi) mo*	(私)も

GRAMMAR

Greetings & Civilities

Greetings

Good morning.
   o-hayō gozai masu   お早うございます
Good afternoon.
   konnichi wa   今日は(こんにちは)
Good evening.
   komban wa   今晩は(こんばんは)

People nod or bow when greeting each other, saying goodbye, apologising, and showing gratitude. The deeper the bow, the deeper the respect for the other person's age or status. Sometimes, when receiving honoured guests, the woman of the household will kneel on the floor and bow with her head almost touching the ground. You can return the gesture, although an upright bow is also acceptable.

Remember you should normally take off your shoes when you enter someone's home.

Attracting Someone's Attention

Excuse me. すみません
sumi masen

Excuse me please.
shitsurei shimasu 失礼します

Ah ...
anō ... あのう...

Hey you!
chotto! ちょっと！

Say *moshi moshi* to attract a waiter's attention or when you pick up the phone.

To see if anyone's around – for example, in an empty shop or office – use the expression *go-men kudasai*.

Excuse me, could you come here please?
sumi masen ga, chotto kite kudasai すみませんが、ちょっと来て下さい

Could you give me a hand?
tetsudatte itadake masen ka? 手伝って頂けませんか？

Could you do me a favour?
o-negai deki masen ka? お願いできませんか？

Could you take a photo?
shashin o totte itadake masen ka? 写真を撮って頂けませんか？

Introductions

This is Mr/Mrs/Ms (Smith).
kochira wa (Sumisu) san desu こちらは(スミス)さんです

My name is (Smith).
watashi wa (Sumisu) desu 私は(スミス)です

Pleased to meet you.
dōzo yoroshiku どうぞよろしく

Pleased to meet you too.
  hajime mashite, kochira koso　　はじめまして、こちらこそ
  dōzo yoroshiku　　どうぞよろしく

Seeing Someone Again
It's been a long time (since I last saw you).
  o-hisashi buri desu　　お久しぶりです
How are you (feeling)?
  go-kigen wa ikaga desu ka?　　ご機嫌はいかがですか？
I'm fine, thank you; and you?
  o-kage sama de, genki desu;　　お蔭様で、元気です
  anata wa?　　あなたは？
I'm fine too, thank you.
  watashi mo genki desu, dōmo　　わたしも元気です
  arigatō gozai masu　　どうもありがとうございます
How are you? (informal)
  o-genki desu ka?　　お元気ですか？

Goodbyes
Goodbye.
  sayōnara　　さようなら
  or *bai bai*　　バイバイ！
Good night.
  o-yasumi nasai　　お休みなさい

Use *mata ai mashō* or *mata* when you will probably meet again soon.

See you!
  sore dewa mata　　それでは また
See you! (informal)
  dewa mata　　では また

See you! (very informal)
ja mata　　　　　　　　　　じゃ また

See you tomorrow.
dewa mata ashita　　　　　　では またあした

See you next week.
dewa mata raishū　　　　　　では また来週

Some other useful parting expressions:

Please come again.
mata kite kudasai　　　　　　また来て下さい

Take care.
ki o tsukete kudasai　　　　　気をつけて下さい

Best regards.
go-kigen yō　　　　　　　　　ご機嫌よう

Have a good trip.
yoi go-ryokō o　　　　　　　よい ご旅行を

I will come again.
mata ki masu　　　　　　　　また 来ます

Please (also) give my regards to
Mr/Mrs/Ms Suzuki.
Suzuki san ni (mo) yoroshiku　鈴木さんに（も）
o-tsutae kudasai　　　　　　よろしくお伝え下さい

Requests
Asking For Something

A polite way to ask for something is to say ... *o kudasai*, roughly
equivalent to 'Please give me ...'.

Please give me this/that.
(kore)/(sore) o kudasai　　　（これ）／（それ）を下さい

Please give me a (cup of tea).
(o-cha) o kudasai （お茶）を下さい

Other Common Requests & Offers
Please come in.
dōzo o-hairi kudasai どうぞお入り下さい
or *dōzo haitte kudasai* どうぞ入って下さい
Please sit down.
o-suwari kudasai おすわり下さい
Please wait (a while).
(shōshō) o-machi kudasai （少々）お待ち下さい
Please eat.
meshiagatte kudasai 召上がって下さい
Please eat. (informal)
tabete kudasai 食べて下さい
Please hurry.
isoide kudasai 急いで下さい
Please show me (the ticket).
(kippu o) misete kudasai （切符を）見せて下さい

You'll often hear the phrase *o-saki ni dōzo*, which along with a hand gesture – for example, towards a door – means 'Please go first'.

Thank You
Thank you.
dōmo arigatō どうもありがとう
Thank you very much.
dōmo arigatō gozai mashita どうもありがとうございました
Thanks. (informal)
dōmo どうも

Thank you for your courteousness.
    dōmo go-teinei ni   どうもご丁寧に
Thank you for your kindness.
    dōmo go-shinsetsu ni   どうもご親切に

The usual reply is:

It's a pleasure.
    dō itashi mashite   どういたしまして

Apologies
Sorry.
    sumi masen   すみません
    or *go-men nasai*   ごめんなさい
I'm very sorry.
    hontōni sumi masen   本当にすみません
    or *mōshiwake ari masen*   申し訳ありません

Please forgive me.
    yurushite kudasai   許して下さい

(I've) made a mistake.
    machigae mashita   間違えました

Sorry to keep you waiting.
    taihen o-matase shi mashita   大変お待たせしました

In reply you should say:

Never mind.
    daijōbu desu   大丈夫です

Civilities
Forms of Address

Excuse me, may I ask your name?
    shitsurei desu ga, o-namae wa   失礼ですが、お名前は何と
    nan to osshai masu ka?   おっしゃいますか？

May I ask who this is?
    dochira sama desu ka?   どちら様ですか？

My surname is (Smith).
    watashi wa (Sumisu) desu   私は（スミス）です

Traditionally, only close friends and children call each other by their first names, and so a new Japanese acquaintance will normally just tell you their surname. When addressing a person, follow their surname with *san*, equivalent to any of the English titles Mr, Mrs, Miss and Ms. For example, Ms Suzuki becomes *Suzuki san*.

As *san* shows respect, it is never used to refer to yourself, your family, or even colleagues from work when talking about them to outsiders. For example, if someone is asking for your colleague

Mr Tanaka and he's not around, you would say 'Tanaka (instead of Tanaka *san)* is not here'. This applies even when talking about your boss!

Since the word *san* does not indicate gender, in order to refer to a particular member of a family, such as 'Mrs Tanaka', Japanese will say *tanaka san no okusan* 'Tanaka *san*'s wife'.

Sama is a very respectful form of *san*: for example, Honourable Guest is *o-kyaku sama* and God is called *kami sama*. The cliché 'the customer is always right' pales in comparison with the Japanese phrase *o-kyaku sama wa kami sama desu*, 'the customer is God'!

You can also replace *san* with a more specific word referring to a person's occupation. For example, *sensei* is used for professionals such as teachers, doctors and lawyers. Mr Yamada, the lawyer, can be called *Yamada sensei*. It's also quite acceptable to address someone as *sensei* without their surname. Other titles used in a similar way include:

company president	*kai chō*	会長
divisional chief	*bu chō*	部長
general manager	*sha chō*	社長
manager	*ka chō*	課長
married woman	*okusan*	奥さん
or *okusana*		奥様

Small children are often addressed by their first name plus *chan*.

Surnames

Most Japanese surnames are written as two *kanji* (Chinese characters). However, some have only one, and some have three or more. Of the thousands of Japanese surnames, *Suzuki* is the most common. Here are some others you may come across:

Abe	阿部
Azuma	吾妻
Itō	伊藤
Kishi	岸
Kondō	近藤
Matsuda	松田
Mori	森
Satō	佐藤
Shōji	東海林
Suzuki	鈴木
Takahashi	高橋
Tanaka	田中
Watanabe	渡辺
Yamada	山田

Crests

Some businesses and families have their own crest or insignia such as a flower, a bird, or a Chinese character. A family will weave the insignia onto their formal kimonos, while a restaurant, for example, will display it on lanterns, fabrics and the *noren*, a cloth sign hanging at the front door which symbolises the shop's long-standing reputation.

Hollyhock leaves are used for the crest of the Kamigamo and Shimogamo Shrines in Kyoto and also of the Tokugawa family. The Imperial Crest and the national symbol is a chrysanthemum with 16 petals – you can see it on the front page of Japanese passports.

crest	*ka-mon*	家紋
chrysanthemum crest	*kiku no mon*	菊の紋
hollyhock crest	*aoi no mon*	葵の紋
paulownia crest	*kiri no mon*	桐の紋

Body Language & Gestures

It is best to avoid public displays of emotion, especially anger. Sometimes Japanese will smile when they are confused or embarrassed.

Pointing with your finger may offend; it is more polite to use your hand, with the palm facing upwards. (Ironically, the index finger is called *hitosashi-yubi*, literally 'the finger for pointing at people'!) To indicate yourself you should point at your nose. Waving your hand in front of your nose, similar to the gesture when smelling something unpleasant, means 'no'.

People rub their ears with their thumb and index finger after they have held something hot, like a cup of tea.

Money is shown by making a circle with your index finger and thumb. Your thumb by itself can represent your father, and your little finger can mean your boyfriend or girlfriend.

When eating, Japanese normally do not pour their own beer or wine. You should fill everyone else's cup or glass, and wait for someone to fill yours.

Married couples do not traditionally show affection towards each other in public. There still exists an old custom where a wife must walk half a step behind her husband. However, walking hand-in-hand is becoming more common among young people.

Small Talk

Meeting People

Like anywhere, you can break the ice by asking a simple question. Smiling creates a good impression in any situation.

Start with *sumi masen ga, ...*, 'Excuse me, ...', and try asking:

What time is it?
   ima nanji desu ka?   今 何時ですか？

May I use your lighter?
   raitā o kashite itadake   ライターを 貸して
   masen ka?   頂けませんか？

Would you please take a picture for me?
   shashin o totte itadake masen ka? 写真を撮って頂けませんか？

I am going to ...; how about you?
   watashi wa ... e iki masu ga,   私は...へ 行きますが、
   anata wa?   あなたは？

What is this/that?
   (kore)/(sore) wa nan desu ka?   (これ)/(それ)は何ですか？

Are you Japanese?
   nihon no kata desu ka?   日本の方ですか？

Are you a student?
   gaku sei san desu ka?   学生さんですか？

Where is the ...?
   ... wa dochira desu ka?   ...はどちらですか？

How do you say these characters?
   kore wa nihongo de nan to   これは日本語で
   yomi masu ka?   何と読みますか？

Countries & Areas

What country do you come from?
> *dochira no kuni kara ki mashita ka?*   どちらの国から 来ましたか？

Where are you from?
> *doko kara ki mashita ka?*   どこから 来ましたか？

What nationality are you?
> *o-kuni wa dochira desu ka?*   お国はどちらですか？

Just add the word *-jin* 'person' after the name of the country to express your nationality:

I am (American).
> *watashi wa (amerika)-jin desu*   私は(アメリカ)人です

America	*amerika*	アメリカ
	or *bei koku*	米国
Australia	*ōsutoraria*	オーストラリア
Austria	*ōsutoria*	オーストリア
Bangladesh	*banguradeshu*	バングラデシュ
Belgium	*berugī*	ベルギー
Brazil	*burajiru*	ブラジル
Cambodia	*kambojia*	カンボジア
Canada	*kanada*	カナダ
China	*chūgoku*	中国
Denmark	*demmāku*	デンマーク
Egypt	*ejiputo*	エジプト
foreign country	*gaikoku*	外国
France	*furansu*	フランス
Germany	*doitsu*	ドイツ
Greece	*girishia*	ギリシア

Holland	*oranda*	オランダ
Hong Kong	*hon kon*	香港
India	*indo*	インド
Indonesia	*indoneshia*	インドネシア
Italy	*itaria*	イタリア
Japan	*nihon*	日本
Korea	*kankoku*	韓国
Laos	*raosu*	ラオス
Malaysia	*marēshia*	マレーシア
New Zealand	*nyūjīrando*	ニュー・ジーランド
Peru	*perū*	ペルー
Philippines	*firipin*	フィリピン
Portugal	*porutogaru*	ポルトガル
Russia	*roshia*	ロシア
Singapore	*shingapōru*	シンガポール
Spain	*supein*	スペイン
Switzerland	*suisu*	スイス
Thailand	*tai*	タイ
Turkey	*toruko*	トルコ
UK	*igirisu*	イギリス
	or *ei-koku*	英国
USA	*amerika*	アメリカ
Vietnam	*betonamu*	ベトナム

Are you (American)?
  anata wa (amerika-jin) desu ka? あなたは(アメリカ人)ですか?
I am not (American), I am (French).
  watashi wa (amerika-jin) dewa 私は(アメリカ人)
  ari masen, watashi wa (furansu- ではありません
  jin) desu 私は(フランス人)です

I come from (Hong Kong).
watashi wa (hon kon) kara　　　私は（香港）から
ki mashita　　　来ました

You may also add the word *-go* 'language' to the name of a country to signify the language spoken there.

I speak (Spanish) and (French).
watashi wa (supein-go) to　　　私は（スペイン語）と
(furansu-go) o hanashi masu　　　（フランス語）を 話します

Chinese	*chūgoku-go*	中国語
English	*ei-go*	英語
French	*furansu-go*	フランス語
German	*doitsu-go*	ドイツ語
Japanese	*nihon-go*	日本語
Portuguese	*porutogaru-go*	ポルトガル語
Russian	*roshia-go*	ロシア語
Spanish	*supein-go*	スペイン語

Some Useful Words & Phrases

Africa	*afurica*	アフリカ
Antarctic	*nankyoku tairiku*	南極大陸
Asia	*ajia*	アジア
continent	*shū*	洲
country	*kuni*	国
dialect	*hōgen*	方言
Europe	*yōroppa*	ヨーロッパ
foreigner	*gaijin*	外人
foreign language	*gaikoku-go*	外国語
from	*... kara*	...から

island country	*shima guni*	島国
language	*kotoba*	言葉
Middle East	*chūkin tō*	中近東
nationality	*kokuseki*	国籍
North America	*hoku bei*	北米
Oceania	*oseaniya shū*	オセアニア洲
South America	*nam bei*	南米
Southeast Asia	*tōnan ajia*	東南アジア
UN	*kokuren*	国連

What country?	*doko no kuni desu ka?*	どこの国ですか？
What language?	*nani go desu ka?*	なに語ですか？
What nationality?	*nani jin desu ka?*	なに人ですか？

Age

How old are you?
  o-ikutsu desu ka?　　　　　　お幾つですか？
How old is your son/daughter?
  (musuko)/(musume) san wa　　（息子)/(娘)さんは
  o-ikutsu desu ka?　　　　　　お幾つですか？
I'm (25).
  (ni jū go) desu　　　　　　　(25)です

See the Numbers & Amounts chapter for your particular age. You'll see that there are two sets of numbers, called 'Japanese' and 'Chinese' – to express age you can use either set:

She's (six).
(muttsu) desu （六つ）です
or *(rokusai) desu* （六才）です

Special Birthdays

Five birthdays are particularly special in Japan: 60, 70, 77, 88 and 99. The last three have special names (*kiju, beiju* and *hakuju*) as the characters for these numbers resemble those for *ki* happiness, *bei*, rice and *haku*, white.

Zodiac

Each sign of the Oriental zodiac is named after an animal, and lasts for a year, not a month as in Western astrology. Instead of directly asking someone how old they are, you can ask their zodiac sign, from which you can normally work out what year they were born in.

What is your zodiac sign?
anata wa nani toshi desu ka? あなたは なに年ですか？
I was born in the year of the (monkey).
watashi wa (saru) doshi desu 私は（申）年です

SIGNS OF THE ZODIAC

ANIMAL			TRADITIONAL NAME		YEARS
rat	nezumi	鼠	ne	子	1936 1948 1960 1972 1984 1996
ox	ushi	牛	ushi	丑	1937 1949 1961 1973 1985 1997
tiger	tora	虎	tora	寅	1938 1950 1962 1974 1986 1998
rabbit	usagi	兎	u	卯	1939 1951 1963 1975 1987 1999
dragon	tatsu	龍	tatsu	辰	1940 1952 1964 1976 1988 2000
snake	hebi	蛇	mi	巳	1941 1953 1965 1977 1989 2001
horse	uma	馬	uma	午	1942 1954 1966 1978 1990 2002
sheep	hitsuji	羊	hitsuji	未	1943 1955 1967 1979 1991 2003
monkey	saru	猿	saru	申	1944 1956 1968 1980 1992 2004
rooster	tori	鶏	tori	酉	1945 1957 1969 1981 1993 2005
dog	inu	犬	inu	戌	1946 1958 1970 1982 1994 2006
boar	inoshi-shi	猪	i	亥	1947 1959 1971 1983 1995 2007

Occupations

When Japanese introduce themselves, they often mention the name of the company or organisation they work for.

May I ask who this is?
    dochira sama desu ka?   どちら様ですか？
I'm Yamada from (Mitsubishi).
    watashi wa (Mitsubishi) no   私は（三菱）の山田です
    Yamada desu
Where do you work?
    o-tsutome saki wa dochira desu ka? お勤め先はどちらですか？
What is your occupation?
    go-shokugyō wa nan desu ka?   ご職業は何ですか？

I am a/an ...	*watashi wa ... desu*	私は...です
accountant	*kaikei shi*	会計士
actor	*haiyū*	俳優
architect	*sekkei shi*	設計士
artist	*geijutsu ka*	芸術家
businessman	*bijinesu man*	ビジネス・マン
businesswoman	*bijinesu ūman*	ビジネス・ウーマン
carpenter	*daiku*	大工
chef	*chōri shi*	調理師
chemist	*yakuzai shi*	薬剤師
clerk	*jimu in*	事務員
crew member	*jōmu in*	乗務員
(of a ship,	or *norikumi in*	乗組員
plane, train)		
dancer	*odoriko*	踊り子
	or *dansā*	ダンサー
designer	*dezainā*	デザイナー
director (of	*tori shimari*	取締役
a company)	*yaku*	
doctor	*ishi*	医師
driver	*unten shu*	運転手
editor	*henshūsha*	編集者
employee (of a	*kaisha in*	会社員
company)		
engineer	*enjinia*	エンジニア
farmer	*hyakushō*	百姓
fisherman/	*ryōshi*	漁師
woman		
housewife	*shufu*	主婦
interpreter	*tsūyaku*	通訳
journalist	*kisha*	記者
judge	*saiban kan*	裁判官

lawyer	*bengoshi*	弁護士
lecturer	*kōshi*	講師
manager	*manējā*	マネージャー
model	*moderu*	モデル
musician	*ongaku ka*	音楽家
nurse (m)	*kangoshi*	看護士
nurse (f)	*kangosfu*	看護婦
office worker	*jimu in*	事務員
pastor/priest	*bokushi*	牧師
poet	*shijin*	詩人
policeman/	*porisu*	ポリス
woman	or *keisatsu kan*	警察官
politician	*seijika*	政治家
professor	*kyōju*	教授
public servant	*kōmu in*	公務員
salesman	*sērusu man*	セールス・マン
	or *eigyō man*	営業マン
saleswoman	*sērusu ūman*	セールス・ウーマン
scientist	*kagaku sha*	科学者
secretary	*hisho*	秘書
shop assistant	*ten in*	店員
singer	*kashu*	歌手
soldier	*gun jin*	軍人
	or *jieikan*	自衛官
student	*gakusei*	学生
teacher	*kyōshi*	教師
tour conductor	*tenjō in*	添乗員
tourist	*kankō kyaku*	観光客
typist	*taipisuto*	タイピスト
waiter (m)	*uētā*	ウェーター
waiter (f)	*uētoresu*	ウェートレス
writer	*sakka*	作家

SMALL TALK

Some Useful Words

amateur	*amachua*	アマチュア
job	*shigoto*	仕事
occupation	*shokugyō*	職業
part-time job	*arubaito*	アルバイト
	or *pāto*	パート
profession	*puro*	プロ
	or *semmon*	専門
regular job	*honshoku*	本職
retired	*taishoku*	退職
second job	*fuku gyō*	副業
specialist	*semmon ka*	専門家
unemployed	*shitsu gyō*	失業

Religion

The principal religions in Japan are Shinto, Buddhism and Christianity.

Shinto is a polytheistic religion, influenced by Chinese Confucianism and Buddhism. Celebrations for births and weddings centre around Shinto rituals, while funerals are always Buddhist.

Worshippers believe they are purified when they pass under the *torii* ('sacred bird dwelling'), the archway at the entrance of a Shinto shrine.

What is your religion?

anata no shūkyō wa nan desu ka?　あなたの宗教は何ですか？

I am... *watashi wa ... desu*　私は...です

Buddhist	*buk-kyō*	仏教
Catholic	*katorikku kyō*	カトリック教
Christian	*kirisuto kyō*	キリスト教
Hindu	*hinzū kyō*	ヒンズー教
Jewish	*yudaya kyō*	ユダヤ教
Muslim	*isuramu kyō*	イスラム教
Protestant	*purotesutanto*	プロテスタント

I am not religious.

watashi wa mushūkyō desu　私は無宗教です

Some Useful Words

belief	*shinkō*	信仰
believer	*shinja*	信者
Bible	*seisho*	聖書
Buddhist temple	*o-tera*	お寺
cathedral	*dai seidō*	大聖堂
Christian church	*kyōkai*	教会
church	*kyōkai*	教会
Confucianism	*ju kyō*	儒教
god	*kami sama*	神様
mosque	*mosuku*	モスク
pagoda	*sotoba*	卒塔婆(そとば)
religion	*shūkyō*	宗教
shrine	*jinja*	神社
	or *jingū*	神宮
temple	*o-tera*	お寺
Zen	*zen*	禅
Zen meditation	*za zen*	座禅

Family

Are you married?
kekkon shite i masu ka?　　　　　結婚していますか？

I am married.
kekkon shite i masu　　　　　　　結婚しています

I am single.
mada dokushin desu　　　　　　　まだ独身です

Do you have a boyfriend/girlfriend?
(bōifurendo)/(gārufurendo) wa　　（ボーイフレンド）/（ガール
irassha i masu ka?　　　　　　　　フレンド）は いらっしゃいますか？

Yes, I have.
ee, i masu　　　　　　　　　　　　ええ、います

No, I don't.
iie, i masen　　　　　　　　　　　いいえ、いません

How many children do you have?
o-ko sama wa nan-nin desu ka?　　お子様は何人ですか？

How many brothers and sisters
do you have?
go-kyōdai wa nan-nin desu ka?　　ご兄弟は何人ですか？

I have ... (and ...).	... (to ...) ga i masu	...（と...）がいます
a son	*musuko*	息子
a daughter	*musume*	娘
two sons	*futari no musuko*	二人の息子
three daughters	*san-nin no musume*	三人の娘
an older brother	*ani*	兄
an older sister	*ane*	姉
younger brother	*otōto*	弟
younger sister	*imōto*	妹

I don't have any children.
  kodomo wa i masen　　　子供はいません
I don't have any brothers or sisters.
  kyōdai wa i masen　　　兄弟はいません

Family Members

The words you choose will depend on whether you are referring to your own family or someone else's. Never use the word *san* for yourself or someone in your family.

Is this your ...?	... desu ka?	...ですか？
daughter	*musume san*	娘さん
father	*o-tō sama*	お父様
friend	*o-tomodachi*	お友達
husband	*go-shujin*	ご主人
mother	*o-kā sama*	お母様
older brother	*o-nī san*	お兄さん
older sister	*o-nē san*	お姉さん
parents	*go-ryōshin*	ご両親

son	*musuko san*	息子さん
wife	*oku san*	奥さん
younger brother	*otōto san*	弟さん
younger sister	*imōto san*	妹さん

This is my ...	... *desu*	...です
father	*chichi*	父
husband	*shujin*	主人
mother	*haha*	母
wife	*kanai*	家内
friend	*tomodachi*	友達

Some Useful Words

acquaintance	*shiriai*	知合い
aunt	*oba san*	おばさん
brother-in-law	*giri no ani*	義理の兄
cousin	*itoko*	いとこ
divorced	*rikon*	離婚
Father's Day	*chichi no hi*	父の日
father-in-law	*gifu*	義父
grandfather	*sofu*	祖父
grandmother	*sobo*	祖母
Mother's Day	*haha no hi*	母の日
mother-in-law	*gibo*	義母
relative	*shinseki*	親戚
separated	*bekkyo*	別居
sister-in-law	*giri no ane*	義理の姉
sole parent	*kata oya*	片親
uncle	*oji san*	おじさん
widow	*mibōjin*	未亡人

SMALL TALK

Feelings

I am ...	*watashi wa ...*	私は...
angry	*okotte imasu*	怒っています
healthy	*genki desu*	元気です
hungry	*onaka ga suki mashita*	おなかがすきました
thirsty	*nodo ga kawaki mashita*	喉が渇きました
tired	*tsukare mashita*	疲れました
worried	*shimpai desu*	心配です

I am (very) ...	*watashi wa (totemo) ...-i desu*	私は(とても) ...いです
Are you ...?	*anata wa ...-i desu ka?*	あなたは ...い ですか?
I am not (very) ...	*watashi wa (amari) ...-ku nai desu*	私は(あまり) ...くないです

ashamed	*hazukashi-*	恥ずかし
busy	*isogashi-*	忙し
cold	*samu-*	寒
happy	*ureshi-*	嬉し
hot	*atsu-*	暑
in pain	*ita-*	痛
lonely	*sabishi-*	寂し
scared	*kowa-*	恐
tired	*nemu-*	眠
well	*yoroshi-*	よろし

Describing Things

It is ...   ... *desu*   ... です

To form the negative, replace the final -*i* on the adjective with -*ku nai desu*:

It is not ...   ...-*ku nai desu*   ... くないです

cheap	*yasui*	安い
delicious	*oishii*	美味しい
difficult	*muzukashii*	難しい
dirty	*kitanai*	汚い
easy	*yasashii*	易しい
expensive	*takai*	高い
fast	*hayai*	速い
heavy	*omoi*	重い
light	*karui*	軽い
lovely	*kawaii*	可愛い
noisy	*urusai*	煩い
pretty	*utsukushii*	美しい
sad	*kanashii*	悲しい
strange	*okashii*	おかしい
strict	*kibishii*	厳しい
uncommon	*mezurashii*	珍しい
wonderful	*subarashii*	素晴らしい

Interests

It can be seen as rude to be too forthright with your opinions.

What do you like?
 nani ga o-suki desu ka?   何がお好きですか？

What are your hobbies?
go-shumi wa nan desu ka?　　ご趣味は何ですか？

Do you like ...?	... ga o-suki desu ka?	...がお好きですか？
I like ...	watashi wa ... ga suki desu	私は...が好きです
I don't like ...	... wa suki dewa ari masen	...は 好きではありません
animals	dōbutsu	動物
baseball	yakyū	野球
basketball	basuketto bōru	バスケット・ボール
bonsai	bonsai	盆栽
cards	torampu	トランプ

checkers	*go*	碁
	or *igo*	囲碁
chess	*shōgi*	将棋
Chinese food	*chūka ryōri*	中華料理
classical music	*kurashikku*	クラシック
dancing	*dansu*	ダンス
discos	*disuko*	ディスコ
fishing	*sakana tsuri*	魚釣り
flower arranging	*kadō*	華道
	or *ikebana*	生け花
games	*gēmu*	ゲーム
golf	*gorufu*	ゴルフ
hiking	*haikingu*	ハイキング
horse racing	*keiba*	競馬
Japanese food	*nihon ryōri*	日本料理
karaoke	*karaoke*	カラオケ
kabuki	*kabuki*	歌舞伎
mahjong	*mājan*	マージャン
music	*ongaku*	音楽
origami	*origami*	折り紙
playing games	*asobi*	遊び
popular music	*popyurā*	ポピュラー・
	myūjikku	ミュージック
reading	*dokusho*	読書
shopping	*kaimono*	買い物
singing	*uta*	唄
skating	*sukēto*	スケート
skiing	*sukī*	スキー
soccer	*sakkā*	サッカー
sport	*supōtsu*	スポーツ
	or *undō*	運動

| swimming | *suiei* | 水泳 |
| travelling | *ryokō* | 旅行 |

Language Problems

Please speak in English/Japanese.
(ei-go)/(nihon-go) de hanashite kudasai
(英語)/(日本語)で
話して下さい

I don't speak English/Japanese.
(ei-go)/(nihon-go) wa hanashi masen
(英語)/(日本語)は
話しません

I don't understand English/Japanese.
(ei-go)/(nihon-go) wa wakari masen
(英語)/(日本語)は
わかりません

Do you understand English?
ei-go wa wakari masu ka?
英語はわかりますか?

Is there an interpreter?
tsūyaku wa i masu ka?
通訳はいますか?

How do you say that in Japanese/English?
(nihon-go)/(ei-go) de nan to ii masu ka?
(日本語)/(英語)で
何と言いますか?

Please write it in Romanised Japanese.
rōmaji de kaite kudasai
ローマ字で書いて下さい

Please write in Japanese/English.
(nihon-go)/(ei-go) de kaite kudasai
(日本語)/(英語)で
書いて下さい

Could you tell me ... ?
... o oshiete kudasai masen ka?
...を教えて下さいませんか?

Could you please repeat that?
mō ichido hanashi-te kudasai masen ka?
もう一度 話して
下さいませんか?

SMALL TALK

Could you please speak more slowly?

yukkuri hanashi-te kudasai masen ka?　ゆっくり 話して 下さいませんか？

Please point to the phrase in this book.

kono hon ni aru tokoro o sashi-te kudasai　この本にある所を さして下さい

Just a minute.

chotto matte kudasai　ちょっと待って下さい

Let me see if I can find it in this book.

kono hon ni sore o sagashi masu　この本にそれをさがします

Do you understand?

wakari masu ka?　分かりますか？

I understand.

wakari mashita　分かりました

I don't understand.

wakari masen　分かりません

What does this/that mean?

dō iu imi desu ka?　どう言う意味ですか？

Getting Around

Public transport in Japan is clean, safe, and reliable, and operates frequently from early morning until after midnight. If you happen to get lost, maps are available from stations, and you can ask at a *kōban* (police booth) for directions.

Often for no cost, you can get travel information, book tickets and accommodation, and organise car and bicycle hire at a *midori no madoguchi* ('Green Window') at major stations and travel centres.

I'd like to go to ...
... ni iki tai desu   ...に 行きたいです

How do I get to ...?
... ewa dono yō ni ikeba ii desu ka?   ...へはどのように 行けばいいですか?

Which (bus) do I take to get to ...?
... ewa dono (basu) ni nottara ii desu ka?   ...へはどの(バス)に 乗ったらいいですか?

Is there another way to get there?
hoka no michi ga ari masu ka?   他の道がありますか?

What time does the next ... leave/arrive?	*tsugi no ... wa nanji ni (de)/(tsuki) masu ka?*	次の...は何時に (出)/(着き)ますか?
aeroplane	*hikōki*	飛行機
bus	*basu*	バス
ferry	*ferī*	フェリー
monorail	*monorēru*	モノレール
sightseeing bus	*teiki kankō basu*	定期観光バス
subway	*chikatetsu*	地下鉄
train	*densha*	電車
tram (in Tokyo)	*toden*	都電
(in other cities)	*shiden*	市電

Some Useful Words

'Green Window'	*midori no madoguchi*	みどりの窓口
map	*chizu*	地図
police booth	*kōban*	交番
station	*eki*	駅
tourist map	*annaizu*	案内図
travel agency	*ryokōsha*	旅行社
travel centre	*ryokō sentā*	旅行センター

Finding Your Way

Where is the ...?	*... wa dochira desu ka?*	...は どちらですか?
I'd like to go to the ...	*... ni iki tai desu*	...に 行きたいです
airport	*kūkō*	空港
bus stop	*basu tei*	バス停
car park	*chūshajō*	駐車場

entrance	*iri guchi*	入り口
exit	*de guchi*	出口
ferry pier	*ferī noriba*	フェリー乗り場
left-luggage office	*ichiji azukari jo*	一時預かり所
pier	*futō*	埠頭
station	*eki*	駅
subway station	*chikatetsu eki*	地下鉄駅
taxi stand	*takushī noriba*	タクシー乗り場
terminal	*tāminaru*	ターミナル
ticket office		
(general)	*kippu uriba*	切符売り場
(first-class)	*midori no madoguchi*	みどりの窓口
train station	*eki*	駅
travel centre	*ryokō sentā*	旅行センター
waiting room	*machiai shitsu*	待合室
ticket barrier	*kaisatsu guchi*	改札口

Is it far?
  tooi desu ka?　　　　　　　　　　遠いですか？
Yes, it's far.
  ee, tooi desu　　　　　　　　　　ええ、遠いです
It's not that far.
  sonna ni tooku nai desu　　　　そんなに遠くないです
It's quite close.
  chikai desu　　　　　　　　　　近いです
Can I walk there?
  aruite ike masu ka?　　　　　　歩いて行けますか？
How far is it to walk?
  aruite dono kurai kakari　　　　歩いてどのくらい
  masu ka?　　　　　　　　　　かかりますか？

Could you write down the address for me?

jūsho o kaite itadake masen ka? 住所を書いて頂けませんか?

Could you draw a map for me?

chizu o kaite itadake masen ka? 地図を書いて頂けませんか?

Directions

Where is the (ticket office)?

(kippu uriba) wa dochira desu ka? (切符売り場)は どちらですか?'

(... station) is across the road from the bus terminal.

(... eki) wa basu tāminaru no mamukai desu (...駅)はバス・ ターミナルの真向かいです

Go straight ahead, then turn left/right at the next corner.

massugu itte, tsugi no kado o (hidari)/(migi) e magatte kudasai まっすぐ行って、次の角を (左)/(右)へ 曲って下さい

behind	*... no ushiro*	...の後ろ
corner	*kado*	角
direction	*hōkō*	方向
downstairs	*shita*	下
east	*higashi*	東
far away	*tooi*	遠い
in front of	*... no mae ni*	...の前に
inside	*... no naka ni*	...の中に
left	*hidari*	左
middle	*man naka*	眞ん中
nearby	*chikaku*	近く
next to	*... no tonari*	...の隣り
north	*kita*	北

opposite	*mamukai*	真向かい
outside	*soto*	そと
right	*migi*	右
south	*minami*	南
straight	*massugu*	まっすぐ
that direction	*sochira*	そちら
this direction	*kochira*	こちら
train from Tokyo	*kudari densha*	下り電車
train to Tokyo	*nobori densha*	上り電車
upstairs	*ue*	上
west	*nishi*	西

Buying Tickets

Local tickets can be purchased from any station, bus or tram, and ticket machines are also commonly available. Your ticket will be punched or electronically marked when you enter the system, and collected on your way out.

For travelling between cities, you can reserve a seat or a sleeper and purchase an excursion ticket at any ticket office or travel agency. Tickets can also be reserved over the phone.

A Japan Rail Pass gives you unlimited use of Japan Rail services for a set period, but it can only be purchased from a travel agency outside Japan.

adult	*otona*	大人
child	*kodomo*	子供
discount	*waribiki*	割引き
excursion ticket	*shūyū ken*	周遊券
express ticket	*kyūkō ken*	急行券
Green Ticket (first class)	*gurīn ken*	グリーン券

one-way	kata michi	片道
platform ticket	nyūjō ken	入場券
refund	harai modoshi	払戻し
reserved ticket	shitei seki ken	指定席券
return ticket	ōfuku jōsha ken	往復乗車券
season ticket	teiki ken	定期券
sleeper ticket	shindai ken	寝台券
student discount	gaku wari	学割
ticket (general)	kippu	切符
(for trains only)	jōsha ken	乗車券
ticket to/for (Kobe)	(Kōbe) iki no kippu	(神戸)行きの切符
ticket book	kaisū ken	回数券

How much is the fare to ...?
   ... made wa ikura desu ka?   ...までは幾らですか？
(Three) tickets to (Yokohama), please.
   (Yokohama) iki no kippu o   (横浜)行きの切符を
   (sam-mai) kudasai   (３枚)下さい
I'd like an excursion ticket to (Hokkaido).
   (Hokkaidō) shūyūken o o-negai   (北海道)周遊券を
   shi masu   お願いします
Does it stop at (Atami)?
   (Atami) ni wa tomari masu ka?   (熱海)には止まりますか？

advance booking	mae uri	前売り
budget	yosan	予算
direct train	chokkō sha	直行車
fare	unchin	運賃
... Line	... sen	...線

nonsmoking compartment	*kin en sha*	禁煙車
refund	*harai modoshi*	払戻し
seat	*za seki*	座席
sleeper	*shindai*	寝台
timetable	*jikokuhyō*	時刻表
via ...	*... keiyu*	...経由
window seat	*mado gawa no seki*	窓側の席

Air

Even within Japan, most airline staff know several languages, and instructions are generally also written in English.

Where is the check-in counter for (Tokyo)?

> *(Tōkyō) iki no chekku in kauntā wa dochira desu ka?*

（東京）行きのチェック・イン
カウンターはどちらですか?

I'd like a smoking/nonsmoking/window seat.

> *(kitsuen)/(kin en)/(mado gawa no) seki o o-negai shi masu*

（喫煙）/（禁煙）/（窓側の）
席をお願いします

What time does flight number (123) leave?

> *(ichi-ni-san) bin wa itsu shuppatsu shi masu ka?*

（123）便は いつ
出発しますか?

What is the gate number for the flight to (Osaka)?

> *(Ōsaka) iki no tōjō gēto wa nam ban desu ka?*

（大阪）行きの搭乗ゲートは
何番ですか?

I am not feeling well.

> *kibun ga warui desu*

気分が悪いです

aircraft	*hikōki*	飛行機
airport	*kūkō*	空港
airport tax	*kūkō zei*	空港税
airsick bag	*haki bukuro*	吐き袋
air ticket	*kōkūken*	航空券
baggage	*tenimotsu*	手荷物
boarding pass	*tōjōken*	搭乗券
business class	*bijinesu kurasu*	ビジネス・クラス
cabin luggage	*kinai mochikomi nimotsu*	機内持込み荷物
customs	*zeikan*	税関
customs declaration	*zeikan shinkoku*	税関申告
direct flight	*chokkōbin*	直行便
disembarkation card	*nyūkoku kādo*	入国カード
domestic flight	*kokunai bin*	国内便
economy class	*ekonomī kurasu*	エコノミー・クラス
flight number ...	... *bin*	... 便
first class	*ittō*	一等
	or *fāsuto kurasu*	ファースト・クラス
flight attendant (m)	*suchuwādo*	スチュワード
flight attendant (f)	*suchuwādesu*	スチュワーデス
gate	*tōjō guchi*	搭乗口
gate number ...	... *ban gēto*	... 番ゲート
luggage	*nimotsu*	荷物
nonsmoking	*kin en*	禁煙
passport	*pasupōto*	パスポート
	or *ryoken*	旅券
re-confirm	*sai-kakunin*	再確認
standby	*kūseki machi*	空席待ち

stopover (in ...)	*... ni tachiyori*	...に立寄り
to (Tokyo)	*(tōkyō) iki*	（東京）行き
visa	*biza*	ビザ/査証
waiting room	*machiai shitsu*	待合室

Bus

Most buses are termed *wam man basu*, 'one man bus', having only a driver and no conductor. When you board, deposit the fare in a ticket machine, which will give change if necessary. You can also buy pre-paid tickets in a booklet which gives you eleven for the price of ten.

Anyone can board a *gaku basu* 'school bus'. However, while cheap, these tend to run very limited routes, servicing schools and universities as the name suggests.

If you are travelling a short distance, a *kinichi unchin* (fixed fare) is charged. For longer distances there are different fares depending on where you get on and off. When you get on, take a *seiriken* (numbered ticket) from the machine next to the driver, and the stop is stamped on it. When you get off the driver will collect the appropriate money.

Major cities are also connected by highway buses. These are luxurious, with many facilities on board. Generally you need an advance booking, especially for long distances and night journeys.

Which bus goes to (Tokyo Tower)?
   dono basu ga (Tōkyō Tawā) ni iki　どのバスが（東京タワー）に
   masu ka?　行きますか？

Does this bus go to (the *kabuki* theatre)?

kono basu wa (kabuki-za) ni iki masu ka?

このバスは（歌舞伎座）に行きますか？

I want to get off at (the post office).

(yūbinkyoku no mae) de oroshite kudasai

（郵便局の前）で降ろして下さい

Please tell me when we've reached (there).

(asoko) ni tsuitara oshiete kudasai

（あそこ）に着いたら教えて下さい

airport bus	*kūkō basu*	空港バス
bus terminal	*basu tāminaru*	バス・ターミナル
bus stop	*basu tei*	バス停
bus	*basu*	バス
chartered	*kashi kiri*	貸切り
double-decker	*daburu dekkā*	ダブル・デッカー
driver-only bus	*wam man basu*	ワンマン・バス
highway bus	*haiuei basu*	ハイウェイ・バス
night highway bus	*yakō haiuei basu*	夜行ハイウェイ・バス
out-of-service	*kaisō*	回送
reclining seat	*rikurainingu shīto*	リクライニング・シート
shuttle bus	*shatoru basu*	シャトル・バス
sightseeing bus	*kankō basu*	観光バス
(bus) stop	*teiryūjo*	停留所
Super Highdecker	*sūpā haidekkā*	スーパー・ハイデッカー

Train

During peak hour in Tokyo and Osaka, local trains come every two or three minutes to meet the huge demand. Remember that you only have a few seconds to get on or off!

Most long-distance trains have a dining car, and you can buy an *ekiben* ('station lunch box') from kiosks at major stations.

Where is the nearest (subway) station?
moyori no (chikatetsu no) eki wa dochira desu ka?

最寄りの（地下鉄の）駅は
どちらですか？

How many stations before I reach (Shinjuku)?
(Shinjuku) made ato ikutsu desu ka?

（新宿）まで
あと 幾つですか？

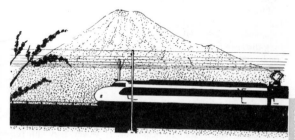

Where should I change for the
(Yamanote Line)?

*doko de (Yamanote sen) ni
norikae masu ka?*

どこで (山の手線) に
乗換えますか？

Can you help me find my seat/sleeper
please?

*watashi no (zaseki)/(shindai) o
sagashite itadake masu ka?*

私の (座席) / (寝台) を
探して頂けますか？

Excuse me, this is my seat.

*sumimasen ga, kore wa watashi
no zaseki desu*

すみませんが、
これは私の座席です

Where is the dining car?

shokudō sha wa dochira desu ka?

食堂車はどちらですか？

Types of Train

bullet train	*shinkansen*	新幹線
direct train	*chokkō*	直行
electric train	*densha*	電車
express	*kyūkō*	急行
fast train	*kaisoku*	快速
limited express	*tokkyū*	特急
locomotive	*kikansha*	機関車
long-distance train	*ressha*	列車
semi-express	*junkyū*	準急
subway	*chikatetsu*	地下鉄
super-express	*chō tokkyū*	超特急

Ferry

Ferries became less important after tunnels and bridges were built
connecting Japan's four main islands. However, they still run
regularly, even as far as Korea, China and Taiwan.

What time does this/the next ferry
depart?

*(kono)/(tsugi no) ferī wa nanji ni
de masu ka?*

（この）/（次の）フェリーは
何時に出ますか？

Taxi

Taxis are readily available from airports, major hotels and stations, and can also be booked over the telephone.

You pay according to the meter, not a pre-arranged price. The fee is somewhat higher early in the morning and late at night. You may also have to pay a levy for using a freeway.

Please go to ...

... ni itte kudasai

...に行って下さい

How long does it take to get to ...?

*... ewa dono kurai kakari
masu ka?*

...へはどのくらい
かかりますか？

Please go to the nearest station/
cinema.

*moyori no (eki)/(eiga kan) ni itte
kudasai*

最寄りの（駅）/（映画館）に
行って下さい

First go to (... station), then (the
airport).

*mazu (... eki) ni itte, soshite
(kūkō) ni itte kudasai*

先ず（...駅）に行って、
そして（空港）に
行って下さい

Please stop here.

koko ni tomete kudasai

ここに止めて下さい

Please stop in front of (that building).

*(ano biru) no mae ni tomete
kudasai*

（あのビル）の前に
止めて下さい

Please stop at the next corner.

tsugi no kado ni tomete kudasai

次の角に止めて下さい

Please hurry.
isoide kudasai 　　　　　　　　急いで下さい
Please slow down.
yukkuri hashitte kudasai 　　　　ゆっくり走って下さい
Please wait here.
koko de matte kudasai 　　　　　ここで待って下さい
Please let me get off here.
koko de oroshite kudasai 　　　　ここで降ろして下さい
How much is it?
ikura desu ka? 　　　　　　　　幾らですか？
Thank you.
arigatō gozai mashita 　　　　　ありがとうございました

automatic door	*jidō doa*	自動ドア
booking	*yoyaku*	予約
extra fare	*warimashi*	割増し
fare meter	*ryōkin mētā*	料金メーター
for hire	*kūsha*	空車
late-night fare	*yakan warimashi ryōkin*	夜間割増し料金
out-of-service	*kaisō*	回送
taxi driver	*takushī untenshu*	タクシー運転手
taxi	*takushī*	タクシー

Renting Cars & Bicycles

The most convenient way to rent a car is to book through a travel agency or travel centre. If your car breaks down you can get free assistance from the Japan Automobile Federation.

Remember that Japanese drive on the left. Parking can be a problem in urban areas.

You can also rent a bicycle from some stations. They come with guide maps identifying places of interest in the area. You can find more information about bicycle rental in Japan Rail timetables.

I'd like to rent a car/bicycle.

(kuruma)/(jitensha) ga kari tai desu （車）/（自転車）が借りたいです

Do you have a map?

chizu ga ari masu ka? 地図がありますか？

How much is it for ...?	... *wa ikura desu ka?*	...は幾らですか？
six hours	*roku jikan*	6 時間
12 hours	*jūni jikan*	12時間
one day	*ichi nichi*	1 日
three days	*mikka kan*	3 日間
one week	*isshū kan*	1 週間
driveaway/ drop-off	*norisute ryōkin*	乗捨て料金

Does that include insurance?

hoken wa fukumarete imasu ka? 保険は含まれていますか？

At the Service Station

Please fill the car up.

mantan ni shite kudasai 満タンにして下さい

Could you check the ...	... *o mite itadake masen ka?*	...を見て頂けませんか？
brakes	*burēki*	ブレーキ
fan belt	*fam beruto*	ファン・ベルト
hazard lamp	*hijō rampu*	非常ランプ
oil	*oiru*	オイル

| radiator | *rajiētā* | ラジエーター |
| tyres | *taiya* | タイヤ |

Traffic Signs

While most signs are international, some important ones are, unfortunately, written in characters!

徐行	**GIVE WAY**
左側通行	**KEEP LEFT**
車両進入禁止	**NO ENTRY**
駐車禁止	**NO PARKING**
駐停車禁止	**NO WAITING**
一方通行	**ONE WAY**
踏切あり	**RAIL CROSSING**
工事中	**ROAD WORKS**
徐行	**SLOW**
止れ！	**STOP!**
一時停止	**STOP!**

Accommodation

Types of Accommodation
Hotels

Western-style *hoteru* are often of luxury standard – and price! They cater for foreign tourists, so you won't have to worry about the language in one of these.

However, knowing some Japanese can be very helpful if you are keen to stay somewhere a bit more unusual.

Japanese Inns

Japanese inns or *ryokan* have mostly Japanese-style rooms with a *shōji* or *fusuma* (wooden-framed sliding paper door), a *tatami* (reed mat), a *futon*, and a *za isu*, a Japanese chair, basically consisting of a cushion and a back support.

Meals are normally included. You may have to share bathroom and toilet facilities.

A cheaper form of traditional accommodation is the *minshuku*, usually a room in a private house. These cater more to Japanese people, and some owners may be unwilling to accept foreigners because of feared language difficulties. However, staying in a *minshuku* can give you a real taste of Japanese life.

Youth Hostels
Japanese *yūsu hosuteru* are usually only open to members of Hostelling International. You may have to prepare your own meals, and within particular times. Some hold activities at night.

Finding Accommodation
It's worth trying to book accommodation in advance. If you are planning to stay in a *minshuku* or *yūsu hosuteru*, you can book over the phone or by post.

Otherwise, tourist desks at airports and railway stations, and even taxi drivers, can be good sources of information regarding where to stay. You may even be approached by a *ryokan* employee at a train station offering you free transport if you stay with them.

Where is ...?	*... wa doko ni ari masu ka?*	...はどこに ありますか？
a hotel	*hoteru*	ホテル
an inn	*ryokan*	旅館
a youth hostel	*yūsu hosuteru*	ユース・ホステル

I'd like a ... hotel/inn.	*...(hoteru)/(ryokan) o sagashite i masu*	... (ホテル)/(旅館)を 探しています
cheap	*yasui*	安い
clean	*kirei na*	綺麗な
good	*ii*	いい
nearby	*kono chikaku no*	この近くの

At the Hotel
Checking In

Do you have a ... ?	*... ga ari masu ka?*	...がありますか？
double room	*daburu rūmu*	ダブル・ルーム
Japanese-style room	*wa shitsu*	和室
room	*heya*	部屋
single room	*shinguru rūmu*	シングル・ルーム
suite	*suīto*	スイート
triple room	*san nin beya*	三人部屋
twin room	*tsuin rūmu*	ツイン・ルーム
Western-style room	*yō shitsu*	洋室

Requirements

I want a room with ...	*... tsuki no heya ga hoshii desu*	...付きの部屋が欲しいです
air conditioning	*ea kon*	エア・コン
a bathroom	*o-furo*	お風呂
a (Western) bed	*beddo*	ベッド
heating	*dambō*	暖房
a refrigerator	*reizōko*	冷蔵庫
a telephone	*denwa*	電話
a television	*terebi*	テレビ
a toilet	*o-tearai*	お手洗い

I'd like a room with a view.
   nagame no ii heya ga hoshii desu   眺めのいい部屋が欲しいです

Negotiation

How much is accommodation only?
su domari wa ippaku ikura desu ka? 素泊まりは一泊 幾らですか？

How much is one night ...	*ippaku ... wa ikura desu ka?*	一泊...は 幾らですか？
with breakfast?	*chōshoku tsuki*	朝食付き
with two meals?	*nishoku tsuki*	二食付き
with three meals?	*sanshoku tsuki*	三食付き

How much is it per person?
hitori ikura desu ka? 一人幾らですか？

Is there a discount for children/students?
(kodomo ryōkin)/(gakusei waribiki) wa ari masu ka? (子供料金)/(学生割引)は ありますか？

Does it include (breakfast)/(a meal)?
(chōshoku)/(shokuji) tsuite imasu ka? (朝食)/(食事) 付いていますか？

Is there anything a bit cheaper?
mō sukoshi yasui no wa ari masu ka? もう少し安いのはありますか？

Please show me the room.
heya o misete kudasai 部屋を見せて下さい

Are there any others?
hoka ni ari masen ka? ほかにありませんか？

I like this/that room.
(kono)/(sono) heya ga suki desu (この)/(その)部屋が好きです

I'll take this/that room.
(kono)/(sono) heya ni shi masu (この)/(その)部屋にします

I'm going to stay   ... *tomari masu*   ...泊まります
for ...

one night	*hito ban*	一晩
two nights	*futa ban*	二晩
four or five days	*shi-go nichi kan*	四五日間
one week	*isshū kan*	一週間

I don't know yet how long I'll stay.

dono kurai tomaru no ka mada   どのくらい泊まるのか
wakari masen   未だ分かりません

Service

Where is the ... ?   ... *wa dochira desu ka?*   ...はどちらですか？

communal bath	*yoku jō*	浴場
dining room	*shokudō*	食堂
elevator	*erebētā*	エレベーター
garden	*niwa*	庭
lounge	*raunji*	ラウンジ
restaurant	*resutoran*	レストラン
room no (123)	*(ichi-ni-san) gō shitsu*	(123)号室
sauna	*sauna*	サウナ
toilet	*o-tearai*	お手洗い

Can I have the key please?

kagi o kudasai   鍵を下さい

My room number is (123).

heya banbō wa (ichi-ni-san) desu   部屋番号は(123)です

Please wake me up at (6.30) tomorrow
morning.

asu asa (roku ji han) ni okoshite   明日朝(6時半)に
kudasai   起して下さい

Please take all my luggage to room
number (123).

<table>
<tr><td>nimotsu o (ichi-ni-san) gō shitsu</td><td>荷物を (123) 号室まで</td></tr>
<tr><td>made motte itte kure masen ka?</td><td>持って行ってくれませんか？</td></tr>
</table>

Can I have ...?	... ga ari masu ka?	...がありますか？
an ashtray	*haizara*	灰皿
clothes hangers	*hangā*	ハンガー
a glass	*gurasu*	グラス
hot water	*o-yu*	お湯
a memo pad	*binsen*	便箋
slippers	*surippa*	スリッパ
tea	*o-cha*	お茶
water	*o-mizu*	お水

Could you please call a taxi?

takushii o yonde kudasai	タクシーを呼んで
masen ka?	下さいませんか？

Are there any ...	*watashi ate no ...*	私宛の...は
for me?	*wa ari masen ka?*	ありませんか？
faxes	*fakkusu*	ファックス
letters	*tegami*	手紙
telegrams	*dempō*	電報
messages	*messēji*	メッセージ

I'm going out for a walk/jogging/
shopping.

(sampo)/(joggingu)/(kaimono) ni	(散歩) / (ジョッギング) /
itte ki masu	(買い物) に行ってきます

I'll be back in 30 minutes/one hour.
   (san jippun)/(ichi jikan) de   (30分)/(1時間)で
   modori masu   戻ります
Please don't disturb me.
   jama shinaide kudasai!   邪魔しないで下さい！
Please keep this in the safe.
   sēfuti bokkusu de azukatte   セーフティ・ボックスで
   kudasai   預かって下さい

Laundry Service

Could I have these   *fuku ... itadake*   服...頂けますか？
clothes ... please?   *masu ka?*
   dry-cleaned   *o dorai kurīningu*   をドライ・クリーニング
   ironed   *ni airon o kakete*   にアイロンをかけて
   washed   *o aratte*   を洗って

I need it ...   *... hoshii desu*   ...欲しいです
   this afternoon   *kyō no gogo*   きょうの午後
   today   *kyōjūni*   きょう中に
   tomorrow   *ashita*   あした
   tonight   *komban*   今晩
   urgently   *dai-shikyū*   大至急

Is my laundry ready?
   watashi no sentaku mono wa   私の洗濯物は
   dekite i masu ka?   出来ていますか？
There's one item missing.
   ichi-mai ari masen   一枚ありません

Requests & Complaints

The room needs to be cleaned.
    heya o sōji shite kudasai   部屋を掃除して下さい

Please change the sheets and pillow case.
    shītsu to makurakabā o torikaete シーツと枕カバーを
    kudasai   取替えて下さい

I don't like this/that room.
    (kono)/(sono) heya wa suki   (この)/(その)部屋は
    dewa arimasen   好きではありません

Can you give me a different room?
    betsu no heya ni torikaete   別の部屋に取替えて
    kudasai masen ka?   下さいませんか？

The toilet is blocked.
    toire ga tsumatte i masu   トイレが 詰まっています

It smells.
    nioi ga shi masu   匂いがします

The door is locked.
    doa no jō ga kakatte i masu   ドアの錠が かかっています

Please have it fixed as soon as possible.
    dai-shikyū naoshite kudasai   大至急 直して下さい

It's too ...	... -*sugi masu*	...過ぎます
big	*ooki*	大き
cold	*samu*	寒
dark	*kura*	暗
dirty	*kitana*	汚
expensive	*taka*	高
far away	*too*	遠
hot	*atsu*	暑

| noisy | *urusa* | 煩 |
| small | *chiisa* | 小さ |

The ... doesn't work.	*... ga tsukae masen*	...が使えません
electricity	*denki*	電気
light	*raito*	ライト
shower	*shawā*	シャワー
tap	*jaguchi*	蛇口
telephone	*denwa*	電話
TV	*terebi*	テレビ

I can't open/close the ...	*... wa (ake)/(shime) rare masen*	...は(開け)/(閉め)られません
curtain	*kāten*	カーテン
door	*doa*	ドア
wardrobe	*wādorōbu*	ワードローブ

I can't turn on the ...	*... ga tsuki masen*	...がつきません
air conditioning	*kūrā*	クーラー
heater	*hītā*	ヒーター
light	*raito*	ライト
shower	*shawā*	シャワー

Checking out

| I would like to check out ... | *... chekku auto shitai desu* | ...チェック・アウトしたいです |

I am leaving ...	... tachi masu	...発ちます
now	ima	今
tomorrow	asu	明日
tomorrow morning	asu no asa	明日の朝
in a while	mō sugu	もうすぐ

I would like to pay by cash/credit card.
(genkin)/(kurejitto kādo) de harai masu　(現金)/(クレジット・カード)で払います

Can I leave my luggage here?
nimotsu o azukatte itadake masen ka?　荷物を預かって頂けませんか?

I'm returning ...	... mata ki masu	...又 来ます
tomorrow	asu	明日
in two or three days	ni-san nichi go	二三日後
next week	rai shū	来週

Thank you for your hospitality.
taihen o-sewa ni nari mashita　大変お世話に なりました

Some Useful Words

babysitter	bebī shittā	ベビー・シッター
baggage	nimotsu	荷物
balcony	barukonī	バルコニー
bathroom	furo ba	風呂場
bed	beddo	ベッド
bill	kanjōsho	勘定書
blanket	mōfu	毛布

candle	*rōsoku*	ろうそく
chair	*isu*	椅子
cot	*kotto*	コット
curtain	*kāten*	カーテン
dining room	*dainingu rūmu*	ダイニング・ルーム
duty manager	*shihai nin*	支配人
electricity	*denki*	電気
elevator	*erebētā*	エレベーター
foyer	*robī*	ロビー
front desk	*furonto*	フロント
glass	*gurasu*	グラス
iron	*airon*	アイロン
key	*kagi*	鍵
laundry	*sentaku mono*	洗濯物
light bulb	*denkyū*	電球
lock	*jōmae*	錠前
lounge	*raunji*	ラウンジ
massage	*messēji*	メッセージ
	or *dengon*	伝言
mini bar	*mini bā*	ミニ・バー
mirror	*kagami*	鏡
morning call	*mōningu kōru*	モーニング・コール
porter	*pōtā*	金庫
refrigerator	*reizōko*	冷蔵庫
registration card	*tōroku kādo*	登録カード
room service	*rūmu sābisu*	ルーム・サービス
safe	*kinko*	ポーター
	or *sēfuti bokkusu*	セーフティ・ボックス
sauna	*sauna*	サウナ
sheet	*shītsu*	シーツ
shower	*shawā*	シャワー

sleeping bag	*surīpingu baggu*	スリーピング・バッグ
	or *nebukuro*	寝袋
soap	*sekken*	石鹸
suitcase	*sūtsu kēsu*	スーツ・ケース
suite	*suīto*	スイート
swimming pool	*pūru*	プール
telephone	*denwa*	電話
television	*terebi*	テレビ
tip	*chippu*	チップ
toilet	*o-tearai*	お手洗い
toilet paper	*toiretto pēpā*	トイレット・ペーパー
towel	*taoru*	タオル
valuables	*kichōhin*	貴重品
visitor	*hōmon kyaku*	訪問客

In a *ryokan* or *minshuku*

basin	*semmen ki*	洗面器
bathrobe	*yukata*	浴衣
cupboard	*oshiire*	押入れ
cushions	*zabuton*	座布団
folding screen	*byōbu*	屏風
foyer	*fumikomi*	踏込み
front door	*genkan*	玄関
futon cover	*kake buton*	掛け布団
mattress	*shiki buton*	敷き布団
ornamental alcove	*toko no ma*	床の間
padded gown	*tanzen*	丹前
pillow	*makura*	枕
pillowcase	*makurakabā*	枕カバー
registration card	*yado chō*	宿帳
sandals	*zōri*	草履

sheet	*shītsu*	シーツ
	or *shiki fu*	敷布
short gown	*haori*	羽織
sliding paper door	(translucent) *shōshi*	障子
	(opaque) *fusuma*	襖
teapot	*kyūsu*	急須
wooden clogs	*geta*	下駄

Around Town

At the Bank

Credit cards are accepted throughout Japan. Travellers' cheques can
be exchanged in most banks, department stores and large shops.

Some banks in airports are open 24 hours a day. Most bank
staff know some English.

Where is the nearest bank?
*moyori no ginkō wa dochira
desu ka?*
最寄りの銀行は
どちらですか?

I'd like to change (this)/($500) into
yen.
*(kore)/(go hyaku doru) o en ni
kaete kure masen ka?*
(これ)/(500ドル)を円に
替えてくれませんか?

I'd like to change (yen) into (US
dollars).
*(nihon en) o (bei doru) ni kaete
kure masen ka?*
(日本円)を(米ドル)に
替えてくれませんか?

Can I cash traveller's cheques?
*toraberāzu chekku o genkin ni
shite kure masen ka?*
トラベラーズ・チェック
を 現金にしてくれませんか?

What is today's exchange rate?
*kyō no kansan rēto wa ikura desu
desu ka?*
今日の換算レートは
幾らですか?

Foreign exchange is on the
(second) floor.
gaikoku kawase wa (ni) kai desu
外国為替は(2)階です

| account | *kōza* | 口座 |
| amount | *kingaku* | 金額 |

90

ATM (Automatic Teller Machine)	*genkin jidō hikidashi ki*	現金自動引出機
balance	*zandaka*	残高
bank	*ginkō*	銀行
bank draft	*ginkō kogitte*	銀行小切手
banknote	*satsu*	札
cashcard	*kyasshu kādo*	キャッシュ・カード
cash	*genkin*	現金
cheque	*kogitte*	小切手
cheque account	*tōza yokin*	当座預金
coins	*koin*	コイン
credit card	*kurejitto kādo*	クレジット・カード
deposit	*yokin*	預金
draft	*tegata*	手形
exchange	*ryōgae*	両替
exchange rate	*kawase rēto*	為替レート
	or *kansan rēto*	換算レート
foreign currency	*gaika*	外貨
handling charge	*tesūryō*	手数料
identification card	*mibun shōmei sho*	身分証明書
interest	*kinri*	金利
loan	*rōn*	ローン
money	*o-kane*	お金
money order	*kawase*	為替
passbook	*techō*	手帳
postal order	*yūbin kawase*	郵便為替
remittance	*sōkin*	送金
savings account	*futsū yokin*	普通預金
signature	*sain*	サイン
	or *shomei*	署名
small change	*kozeni*	小銭

telegraphic transfer	*denshin sōkin*	電信送金
teller counter	*madoguchi*	窓口
term deposit	*teiki yokin*	定期預金
travellers' cheque	*ryokō kogitte*	旅行小切手
	or *toraberāzu chekku*	トラベラーズ・チュック
withdrawal	*hiki dashi*	引出し

Currency

Australian $	*ōsutoraria doru*	オーストラリア・ドル
Canadian $	*kanada doru*	カナダ・ドル
Deutschmarks	*maruku*	マルク
English £	*pondo*	ポンド
French francs	*furan*	フラン
Hong Kong $	*hon kon doru*	香港ドル
Japanese ¥	*nihon en*	日本円
US $	*bei doru*	米ドル
	or *amerika doru*	アメリカ・ドル

At the Post Office

When sending mail, it's best to write all English words in block letters to avoid misunderstandings!

Post offices generally have cable and fax services, and sell commemorative stamps and first-day covers, worth considering as souvenirs.

I'd like (three) ¥100 stamps.
   hyaku-en kitte o (sam-mai)   100円切手を(3枚)下さい
   kudasai

How much is it?		
ikura desu ka?		幾らですか？

I would like to send a/an ... to (Canada).	*... o (kanada) ni okuri tai desu*	...を(カナダ)に送りたいです
aerogram	*kōkū shokan*	航空書簡
cable	*dempō*	電報
card	*kādo*	カード
Christmas card	*kurisumasu kādo*	クリスマス・カード
express mail	*sokutatsu*	速達
fax	*fakkusu*	ファックス
letter	*tegami*	手紙
parcel	*ko-zutsumi*	小包み
picture postcard	*e-hagaki*	絵葉書き
postal order	*yūbin kawase*	郵便為替
postcard	*hagaki*	葉書き

Are there any restrictions regarding ...?	*... no seigen wa ari masu ka?*	...の制限はありますか？
size	*saizu*	サイズ
thickness	*atsusa*	厚さ
weight	*jūryō*	重量

Some Useful Words

address	*jūsho*	住所
aerogram	*kōkū shokan*	航空書簡
air mail	*kōkū bin*	航空便
certified mail	*haitatsu shōmei yūbin*	配達証明郵便

commemorative stamp	*ki nen kitte*	記念切手
contents	*nakami*	中身
domestic mail	*kokunai yūbin*	国内郵便
envelope	*fūtō*	封筒
express mail	*sokutatsu*	速達
	or *ekisupuresu*	エキスプレス
GPO	*chūō yūbinkyoku*	中央郵便局
insurance	*hoken*	保険
letter box	*yūbin bako*	郵便箱
mailbox	*posuto*	ポスト
outside Tokyo	*tafuken*	他府県
PO box	*shisho bako*	私書箱
postcode	*yūbin bangō*	郵便番号
post office	*yūbin kyoku*	郵便局
poste restante	*tomeoki*	留置き
printed matter	*insatsu butsu*	印刷物
registered cash mail	*genkin kaki tome*	現金書留め
registered mail	*kaki tome*	書留め
stamp	*kitte*	切手
standard size	*teikei*	定型
surface mail	*funa bin*	船便
to/for (Germany)	*(doitsu) muke*	(ドイツ)向け
to/within Tokyo	*tokunai*	都区内

Telephone

Public phones often accept phone cards, which can be bought from vending machines and some shops. Operators generally speak English if you need help calling overseas.

AROUND TOWN

area code	*shigai kyokuban*	市外局番
collect call	*korekuto kōru*	コレクト・コール
country code	*kuni bangō*	国番号
dial	*daiyaru*	ダイヤル
direct dial	*dairekuto daiyaru*	ダイレクト・ダイヤル
directory	*denwa chō*	電話帳
engaged	*hanashi chū*	話し中
extension number	*naisen bangō*	内線番号
international call	*kokusai denwa*	国際電話
local call	*shinai denwa*	市内電話
long-distance call	*chōkyori denwa*	長距離電話
mobile phone	*mōbiru denwa*	モービル電話
operator	*kōkanshu*	交換手
out of order	*koshō*	故障
public phone	*kōshū denwa*	公衆電話
return call	*orikae shi denwa*	折返し電話
telephone	*denwa*	電話
telephone booth	*denwa bokkusu*	電話ボックス
telephone card	*terehon kādo*	テレホン・カード
telephone charge	*denwa ryōkin*	電話料金
telephone number	*denwa bangō*	電話番号
wrong number	*machigai denwa*	間違い電話
White Pages	*howaito pēji*	ホワイト・ページ
Yellow Pages	*ierō pēji*	イエロー・ページ

There are three Japanese companies which handle international calls:

IDC *kokusai dejitaru tsūshin* (prefix: 0061)	国際デジタル通信
ITJ *nihon kokusai tsūshin* (0041)	日本国際通信
KDD *kokusai denshin denwa* (001)	国際電信電話

AROUND TOWN

Sightseeing

Excuse me, what's
this/that?

sumimasen ga, (kore)/　すみませんが、(これ)/
(sore) wa nan desu ka?　(それ)は 何ですか?

Do you have a tourist
map?

annai zu wa　案内図は
ari masen ka?　ありませんか?

Am I allowed to take
photos here?

koko de shashin o　ここで写真を撮っても
tottemo ii desu ka?　いいですか?

What time does it
open/close?

nanjini (ake)/　何時に(開け)/
(shime) masu ka?　(閉め)ますか?

How much is ... ?　*... wa ikura desu ka?*　…は 幾らですか?

the admission fee	*nyūjō ryō*	入場料
	or *nyūen ryō*	入園料
	or *haikan ryō*	拝観料
a guidebook	*gaido bukku*	ガイド・ブック
	or *annai sho*	案内書
a postcard	*e-hagaki*	絵葉書き
this/that	*kore/sore*	(これ)/(それ)
a tourist map	*annai zu*	案内図

Things to See

The Japanese Government identifies various grades of sights,
including: *jūyō bunka zai* 'Important Cultural Properties', and
kokuhō 'National Treasures'.

AROUND TOWN

aquarium	*suizoku kan*	水族館
art gallery	*bijutsu kan*	美術館
botanic garden	*shokubutsu kōen*	植物公園
bridge	*hashi*	橋
building	*tatemono*	建物
castle	*shiro*	城
church	*kyōkai*	教会
farm	*bokujō*	牧場
Imperial Palace	*kōkyo*	皇居
Japanese garden	*nihon teien*	日本庭園
lookout	*miharashi dai*	見晴台
market	*ichiba*	市場
museum	*hakubutsu kan*	博物館
pagoda	*tō*	塔
park	*kōen*	公園
ruins	*iseki*	遺跡
sculpture	*chōkoku*	彫刻
shrine	*jinja*	神社
shrine archway	*torii*	鳥居
statue	*dōzō*	銅像
temple	*o-tera*	お寺
theatre	*geki jō*	劇場
tower	*tawā*	タワー
university	*dai gaku*	大学
zoo	*dōbutsu en*	動物園

Some Useful Words

additional charge	*tsuika ryōkin*	追加料金
afternoon tour	*gogo no tsuā*	午後のツアー
ancient	*kodai*	古代
city tour	*shinai kankō*	市内観光
course	*kōsu*	コース

day trip	*higaeri*	日帰り
English-speaking guide	*eigo no gaido*	英語のガイド
excursion ticket	*shūyūken*	周遊券
fare	*unchin*	運賃
free (of charge)	*muryō*	無料
history	*rekishi*	歴史
... included	*... komi*	...込み
map	*chizu*	地図
meal included	*shokuji tsuki*	食事付き
night tour	*ibuningu tsuā*	イブニング・ツアー
	or *naito tsuā*	ナイト・ツアー
observe	*kengaku*	見学
one-day tour	*ichinichi tsuā*	一日ツアー
route	*michijun*	道順
sightseeing	*kankō*	観光
	or *yūran*	遊覧
sightseeing bus	*kankō basu*	観光バス
souvenirs	*mingei hin*	民芸品
	or *o-miyage hin*	お土産品
visit	*haikan*	拝観

Entertainment & Nightlife

Among Japanese, the most popular forms of entertainment are movies and *pachinko*, pinball. In all major cities there are numerous discos, cabarets, nightclubs and karaoke bars, but they tend to be expensive.

The famous night views of Nagasaki, Hakodate and Kōbe should not be missed.

Do you like (karaoke)?
   (karaoke) wa o-suki desu ka?   (カラオケ) は お好きですか？
I like (opera).
   (opera) ga suki desu   (オペラ) が好きです

AROUND TOWN

I would like to see a/an ...	*... o mi ni iki tai desu*	...を見に行きたい です
ballet	*barē*	バレー
baseball match	*yakyū no shiai*	野球の試合
baseball night game	*naitā*	ナイター
circus	*sākasu*	サーカス
horse race	*keiba*	競馬
magic show	*kijutsu*	奇術
movie	*eiga*	映画
opera	*opera*	オペラ
show	*shō*	ショー
Sumo match	*sumō*	相撲

I would like to go to a ...	... *ni iki tai desu*	...に行きたいです
casino	*kajino*	カジノ
cinema	*eiga kan*	映画館
concert	*konsāto*	コンサート
dance	*dansu*	ダンス
disco	*disuko*	ディスコ
karaoke bar	*kara oke*	カラオケ
nightclub	*kurabu*	クラブ
pinball parlour	*pachinko*	パチンコ

Sumo Wrestling

An extremely popular traditional sport, *sumō* originated as a religious rite to obtain the blessing of the gods for the year's harvest.

Six *ōzumō*, or 'grand *sumō* tournaments', are held each year across different cities. Competition is limited to 38, each dreaming of becoming a *yokozuna*, 'grand champion', a title held for life.

The wrestlers build up their gigantic bulk with a staple diet of fattening stew called *chanko nabe*. During the match they wear only loincloths. During warm-up they stamp their feet, spit and toss salt around the arena.

The wrestlers pound their starting lines with their fists to indicate that they are ready. The referee signals the start of the match with the call *matta!* and the wrestlers attack, attempting to throw their opponent onto the ground or out of the ring.

Some Useful Words & Terms

arena	*dohyō*	土俵
loincloth	*mawashi*	回し
program	*banzuke hyō*	番付表
referee	*gyōji*	行司
school	*heya*	部屋
stomping	*shiko*	四股
tactics	*waza*	技
tournament	*basho*	場所
wrestler	*rikishi*	力士

chanko nabe　　　ちゃんこ鍋
　the wrestlers' staple food: a rich and fattening stew
dohyōiri　　　土俵入り
　opening ceremony
gīnōshō　　　技能賞
　prize awarded for skill
gumpai　　　軍配
　fan held by the referee as a symbol of his authority
hiki otoshi　　　引落し
　pull down
higashi　　　東
　east end of the arena
kantōshō　　　敢闘賞
　prize awarded for fighting spirit
matta　　　まった
　'Start the match!'
nishi　　　西
　west end of the arena
nokotta　　　のこった
　'Continue!'
oshi taoshi　　　押倒し
　knock or throw down
oshi dashi　　　押出し
　push out of the arena
senshūraku　　　千秋楽
　finishing ceremony
shukunshō　　　殊勲賞
　prize for distinguished achievement
sunakaburi　　　砂かぶり
　front-row seats

tachi mochi　　　　　太刀持ち
　　sword bearer in the opening ceremony
tennōhai　　　　　天皇杯
　　Emperor's Cup, awarded to the grand champion
tsuri dashi　　　　　吊出し
　　carry the opponent out
yori kiri　　　　　寄切り
　　drive out of the arena

Traditional Japanese Entertainment

Traditional performances are considered as much art as entertainment.

Bunraku　　　　文楽

Musical puppet drama accompanied by a *shamisen*, a lute-like instrument with three strings.

jōruri　　　　浄瑠璃
   musical accompaniment
ningyō　　　　人形
   puppet
omo zukai, *ashi zukai* and *hidari zukai*　　面遣い/足遣い/左遣い
   trio of puppeteers operating the performance

Kabuki　　　　歌舞伎

Spectacular musical drama in which both the male and female roles are played by men.

hana michi　　　　花道
   elevated section in front of the stage
mawari butai　　　　まわり舞台
   revolving stage

Nō　　　　能

Type of play involving stylised movement, chanting, and elaborate costumes and masks.

atoza　　　　後座
   space for the orchestra
hashigakari　　　　橋懸り
   suspended entrance to the stage
hayashi　　　　はやし
   musical accompaniment
kyōgen or *aikyōgen*　　狂言/間狂言
   comic interlude between acts

mai   舞
  dance
men or *kamen*   面/仮面
  mask
shite   仕手
  principal actor
yōkyoku or *utai*   謡曲/謡
  chorus

Yose   寄席
Popular theatre.

kōdan   講談
  historical story telling
manzai or *kōshaku*   漫才/講釈
  comic dialogue
naniwa bushi or *rōkyoku* 浪花武士/浪曲
  story-telling and singing
rakugo   落語
  comic story telling

Traditional Music
biwa   琵琶
  four-stringed lute
dōyō   童謡
  children's song
ga gaku   雅楽
  court music
hō gaku   邦楽
  traditional Japanese music

komori uta　　　　　子守り歌
　lullaby
koto or *o-koto*　　　琴/お琴
　thirteen-stringed zither
ko uta　　　　　　　小唄
　short popular song
min yō　　　　　　　民謡
　folk song
naga uta　　　　　　長唄
　epic song
shaku hachi　　　　　尺八
　five-holed bamboo flute
sō kyoku　　　　　　そう曲
　music played on a koto
taiko　　　　　　　太鼓
　drum

Signs

ご注意	**CAUTION**
閉店	**CLOSED**
危険	**DANGER**
手を触れないで下さい	**DO NOT TOUCH**
非常口	**EMERGENCY EXIT**
入り口	**ENTRANCE**
出口	**EXIT**
案内所	**INFORMATION**
入場お断り	**NO ADMITTANCE**
立入り禁止	**NO ENTRY**
フラッシュ禁止	**NO FLASHES**

駐車禁止	**NO PARKING**
撮影禁止	**NO PHOTOGRAPHS**
禁煙	**NO SMOKING**
営業中	**OPEN**
受付	**RECEPTION**
土足厳禁	**TAKE OFF SHOES**
工事中	**UNDER CONSTRUCTION**
火気厳禁	**USE OF FIRE STRICTLY PROHIBITED**

TOILETS

Toilet	*otearai*	お手洗い
Powder Room	*keshō shitsu*	化粧室
Male	*otoko*	男
Female	*onna*	女
Gentlemen	*donogata*	殿方
Ladies	*fujin*	婦人

In the Country

Japan provides many opportunities for 'getting away from it all', especially skiing and mountain climbing. Tourist Information Centres (TIC) can provide you with maps and travel advice.

Weather
Japanese weather is notorious for changing dramatically – it's worth getting updates!

What will the weather be like
(today/tomorrow)?

(kyō/ashita) no tenki wa dō deshō ka?	（きょう）/（あした）の天気は どうでしょうか？

It will be/There
will be ...
(today/tomorrow).

	(kyō/ashita) wa ... deshō	（きょう）/（あした）は ...でしょう
clear	*hare*	晴れ
cloudy	*kumori*	曇り
fine	*ii tenki*	いい天気
fog	*kiri*	霧
heavy rain	*oo ame*	大雨
heavy snow	*oo yuki*	大雪
rain	*ame*	雨
showers	*niwaka ame*	にわか雨
snow	*yuki*	雪
stormy	*arashi*	嵐
wind	*kaze*	風

IN THE COUNTRY

The weather is nice today.

kyō wa ii tenki desu きょうはいい天気です

Will it rain tomorrow?

ashita ame ga furu deshō ka? あした 雨が降るでしょうか？

Some Useful Words

bright	*akarui*	明るい
cloud	*kumo*	雲
dark	*kurai*	暗い
dew	*tsuyu*	露
evening glow	*yūyake*	夕焼け
flood	*kōzui*	洪水

fog	*kiri*	霧
frost	*shimo*	霜
hail	*hyō*	雹
lightning	*inazuma*	稲妻
mist	*kasumi*	霞
mud	*doro*	泥
rain	*ame*	雨
rainbow	*niji*	虹
sky	*sora*	空
smog	*sumoggu*	スモッグ
snow	*yuki*	雪
sunset	*nichi botsu*	日没
temperature	*kion*	気温
thunder	*kaminari*	雷
tornado	*tatsu maki*	竜巻
typhoon	*taifū*	台風
wind	*kaze*	風

Camping & Day Trips

Have you brought the ...?
    ... o motte ki mashita ka?   ...を持ってきましたか？
Should we bring the ...?
    ... o motte itta hō ga ii   ...を持って行った方が
    desu ka?   いいですか？
When do we go?
    itsu iki masu ka?   いつ行きますか？
Where do we meet?
    doko de machiawase mashō ka?   どこで待合わせましょうか？

We will come back ...	*... kaeri masu*	...帰ります
in the evening	*yūgata ni*	夕方に

at (nine) o'clock	*(ku) ji ni*	（9）時に
tomorrow	*asu*	あす
tomorrow evening	*asu no yūgata ni*	あすの夕方に
the day after tomorrow	*asatte*	あさって

backpack	*bakku pakku*	バック・バック
balloon	*barūn*	バルーン
	or *kikyū*	気球
boots	*būtsu*	ブーツ
campfire	*kyampu faia*	キャンプ・ファイア
camping	*kyampingu*	キャンピング
	or *kyampu*	キャンプ
campsite	*kyampu jō*	キャンプ場
caving	*kēbingu*	ケービング
compass	*kompasu*	コンパス
departure time	*shuppatsu jikan*	出発時間
hiking	*haikingu*	ハイキング
insect repellent spray	*mushi yoke supurei*	虫除けスプレイ
knife	*naifu*	ナイフ
map	*chizu*	地図
mountaineering	*yama nobori*	山登り
parachute	*parashūto*	パラシュート
picnic	*pikunikku*	ピクニック
rainwear	*amagu*	雨具
rope	*nawa*	縄
sleeping bag	*surīpingu baggu*	スリーピング・バッグ
	or *nebukuro*	寝袋
sunscreen	*hiyake dome kurīmu*	日焼け止めクリーム

telescope	*bōen kyō*	望遠鏡
tent	*tento*	テント
torch	*kaichū dentō*	懐中電灯
trekking	*torekkingu*	トレッキング
water bottle	*suidō*	水筒

Along the Way

Where are we on this map?
kono chizu de genzai ichi wa doko desu ka?
この地図で 現在位置は どこですか?

It is here (on this map).
(kono chizu dewa) koko desu
(この地図では) ここです

Is it far to ...?
... made wa tooi desu ka?
... までは 遠いですか?

Can we walk to ...?

    ... made wa aruite ike masu ka?   ...までは歩いて行けますか?

Please tell me how to get to ...

    ... made no michi o oshiete   ...までの道を教えて下さい
    kudasai

How far is it from here to ...?

    ... made dono kurai kakari   ...までどのくらい
    masu ka?   かかりますか?

Is there anything to see here?

    kono atari ni mirumono ga ari   このあたりに
    masu ka?   見る物がありますか?

Let's have a rest here.

    koko de yasumi mashō   ここで休みましょう

Can I have a cup of water/tea?

    (o-mizu)/(o-cha) o itadake masu ka?   (お水)/(お茶)を頂けますか?

What's this/that?

    (kore)/(sore) wa nan desu ka?   (これ)/(それ)は何ですか?

Directions

direction	*hōkō*	方向
downhill	*kudari*	下り
east	*higashi*	東
front	*mae*	前
left	*hidari*	左
north-east	*tōhoku*	東北
north-west	*seihoku*	西北
north	*kita*	北
opposite	*mukai*	向かい
rear	*ushiro*	後ろ
right	*migi*	右
south-east	*tōnan*	東南

south-west	*seinan*	西南
south	*minami*	南
uphill	*nobori*	上り
west	*nishi*	西

Which direction?	*dochira desu ka?*	どちらですか？
This direction.	*kochira desu*	こちらです
That direction.	*sochira desu*	そちらです

Geographical Terms

agriculture	*nōgyō*	農業
bay	*wan*	湾
beach	*bīchi*	ビーチ
	or *kaigan*	海岸
bridge	*hashi*	橋
cave	*dōkutsu*	洞窟
cliff	*gake*	崖
the country	*inaka*	田舎
creek	*ogawa*	小川
earthquake	*jishin*	地震
farm	*bokujō*	牧場
forest	*mori*	森
fountain	*funsui*	噴水
geyser	*kanketsu sen*	間けつ泉
harbour	*minato*	港
hill	*oka*	丘
hot spring	*onsen*	温泉
island	*shima*	島
lake	*mizuumi*	湖
landslide	*ji suberi*	地滑り
lighthouse	*tōdai*	灯台

lookout	*miharashi dai*	見晴台
map	*chizu*	地図
mountain	*yama*	山
mountain range	*sam myaku*	山脈
mountain trail	*yama michi*	山道
national park	*kokuritsu kōen*	国立公園
ocean	*kaiyō*	海洋
park	*kōen*	公園
peak	*mine*	峰
peninsula	*hantō*	半島
plain	*heiya*	平野
plateau	*kōgen*	高原
pond	*ike*	池
ricefield	*hatake*	畑
river	*kawa*	川
road	*michi*	道
rock	*iwa*	岩
sea	*umi*	海
spring	*izumi*	泉
stone	*ishi*	石
swamp	*numa*	沼
tide	*shio*	潮
tidal wave	*tsunami*	津波
town	*machi*	町
valley	*tani*	谷
village	*mura*	村
volcano	*kazan*	火山
waterfall	*taki*	滝
wave	*nami*	波
well	*ido*	井戸

IN THE COUNTRY

Animals

animal	*dōbutsu*	動物
badger	*tanuki*	狸(タヌキ)
bear	*kuma*	熊
boar	*inoshishi*	猪(イノシシ)
cat	*neko*	猫
cow	*ushi*	牛
deer	*shika*	鹿
dog	*inu*	犬
frog	*kaeru*	蛙
goat	*yagi*	山羊
horse	*uma*	馬
kangaroo	*kangarū*	カンガルー
koala	*koara*	コアラ
lion	*raion*	ライオン
monkey	*saru*	猿
mouse	*nezumi*	鼠
panda	*panda*	パンダ
pig	*buta*	豚
rabbit	*usagi*	兎
raccoon dog	*tanuki*	狸(タヌキ)
sheep	*hitsuji*	羊
squirrel	*risu*	栗鼠(リス)
tiger	*tora*	虎
wolf	*ookami*	狼

Birds

For Japanese, the crane has traditionally symbolised happiness and long life. In Hiroshima's Peace Memorial Park there is a very moving statue to a girl, who, suffering from radiation caused by the bomb, believed that if she could fold 1000 origami cranes she would survive. Sadly, she did not. However, since then, Japanese school children have left many thousands of folded cranes at the site in memory of her.

bird	*tori*	鳥
chicken	*niwatori*	鶏 (ニワトリ)
crane	*tsuru*	鶴
crow	*karasu*	烏 (カラス)
duck	*kamo*	鴨
eagle	*taka*	鷹
nightingale	*uguisu*	鴬
owl	*fukurō*	梟 (ふくろう)
parrot	*ōmu*	おう鵡
peacock	*kujaku*	孔雀
pelican	*perikan*	ペリカン

penguin	*pengin*	ペンギン
pigeon	*hato*	鳩(はと)
seagull	*kamome*	鴎
sky lark	*hibari*	雲雀(ひばり)
sparrow	*suzume*	雀
swallow	*tsubame*	燕
swan	*haku chō*	白鳥
turkey	*shichimen chō*	七面鳥
woodpecker	*kitsutsuki*	啄木鳥(キツツキ)

Marine Creatures

Being an island country, Japan is surrounded by an abundance of marine life.

abalone	*awabi*	鮑(アワビ)
bonito	*katsuo*	鰹
carp	*koi*	鯉
clam	*hamaguri*	蛤
cod	*tara*	鱈
crab	*kani*	蟹(カニ)
eel	*unagi*	鰻
fish	*sakana*	魚
flounder	*karei*	鰈(カレイ)
globe fish	*fugu*	河豚(フグ)
jellyfish	*kurage*	くらげ
lobster	*ise ebi*	伊勢エビ
mackerel	*saba*	鯖
mussel	*mūru gai*	ムール貝
octopus	*tako*	蛸(タコ)
oyster	*kaki*	牡蠣(カキ)
perch	*suzuki*	鱸(スズキ)

platypus	*kamo no hashi*	カモノハシ
prawn	*kurumaebi*	車エビ
salmon	*sake*	鮭
sardine	*iwashi*	鰯(イワシ)
scallop	*hotategai*	帆立貝
seal	*azarashi*	海豹(アザラシ)
shark	*same*	鮫(さめ)
	or *fuka*	鱶(ふか)
shellfish	*kai*	貝
shrimp	*ebi*	エビ
snapper	*madai*	真鯛
sole	*hirame*	平目
squid	*ika*	烏賊(イカ)
trout	*masu*	鱒(ます)
tuna	*maguro*	鮪
whale	*kujira*	鯨
yellowtail	*aji*	鯵(あじ)

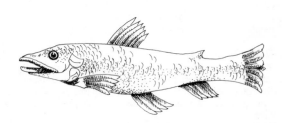

Insects & Reptiles

ant	*ari*	蟻
bee	*hachi*	蜂
beetle	*kabuto mushi*	兜虫
butterfly	*chōchō*	蝶々
cockroach	*gokiburi*	ゴキブリ
crocodile	*wani*	鰐(ワニ)
dragonfly	*tombo*	蜻蛉(トンボ)
flea	*nomi*	蚤
fly	*hae*	蝿
frog	*kaeru*	蛙
grasshopper	*batta*	バッタ
ladybird	*tentōmushi*	てんとう虫
lice	*shirami*	虱
mosquito	*ka*	蚊
moth	*ga*	蛾
silkworm	*kaiko*	蚕
snail	*katatsumuri*	蝸(かたつむり)
snake	*hebi*	蛇
spider	*kumo*	蜘蛛
termite	*shiro ari*	白蟻
turtle	*suppon*	鼈(スッポン)
wasp	*kibachi*	きばち

Plants & Flowers

The cherry blossom *sakura* is one of Japan's national symbols. Each Spring, Japanese celebrate 'flower viewing' or *o-hanami*, when they sing and dance under the blossoming cherry trees.

In Autumn, red maple leaves *kōyō* fill the countryside – a magnificent sight.

Mother's Day *haha no hi* is usually celebrated with carnations.

bamboo	*take*	竹
bracken	*warabi*	蕨（ワラビ）
branch	*eda*	枝
carnation	*kānēshon*	カーネーション
cherry blossom	*sakura*	桜
chrysanthemum	*kiku*	菊
floral art	*kadō*	華道
flower	*hana*	花
flower arrangement	*ike bana*	生け花
forest	*mori*	森
iris	*shōbu*	菖蒲
lily	*yuri*	百合
lotus	*hasu*	蓮
orchid	*ran*	蘭
peony	*botan*	牡丹
pine	*matsu*	松
plum flower	*ume no hana*	梅の花
reed	*ogi*	荻
rose	*bara*	薔薇（バラ）
sunflower	*himawari*	向日葵（ヒマワリ）
tree	*ki*	木
tulip	*chūrippu*	チューリップ
violet	*sumire*	菫

There are three major schools *ryū* of floral art *ikebana*: *ikenobō*, *ōhara* and *sōgetsu*.

Food

Japanese traditionally eat twice a day, and even now most people skip breakfast and only have a light lunch. The main meal of the day is in the evening.

breakfast	chōshoku	朝食
	or asa meshi	朝めし
	or asa gohan	朝御飯
lunch	ranchi	ランチ
	or hiru gohan	昼御飯
dinner	yūshoku	夕食
	or ban gohan	晩御飯
formal dinner	bansan	晩餐
supper	yashoku	夜食
banquet	enkai	宴会
Japanese banquet	kaiseki	会席

At the Restaurant

A table for ... please.
   ... nin o-negai shi masu
   ... 人 お願いします

Can I see the menu please?
   menyū o misete kudasai
   メニューを 見せて下さい

Do you have an English menu?
   ei-go no menyū ga ari masu ka?
   英語のメニューがありますか?

I would like the set menu please.
   setto menyū o o-negai shi masu
   セット・メニューをお願いします

Can you recommend any dishes?
   o-susume no menyū wa ari masu ka?
   お勧めのメニューは ありますか?

Is the (fish) fresh today?
> *kyō no (sakana) wa shinsen desu ka?* 今日の(魚)は 新鮮ですか?

Please give me a knife and a fork.
> *naifu to fōku o kudasai* ナイフとフォークを下さい

The bill please.
> *kanjō o o-negai shi masu* 勘定をお願いします

chef	*itamae*	板前
manager	*shihai nin*	支配人
waiter (m)	*uētā*	ウェーター
waiter (f)	*uētoresu*	ウェートレス

Vegetarian Meals

I am a vegetarian.
> *watashi wa saishoku shugisha desu* 私は菜食主義者です

I don't eat meat.
> *niku rui wa tabe masen* 肉類は 食べません

I like vegetarian food.
> *watashi wa yasai ryōri ga suki desu* 私は野菜料理が 好きです

health food	*kenkō shoku*	健康食
vegetarian meal/	*yasai ryōri*	野菜料理
restaurant	or *shōjin ryōri*	精進料理

Places To Eat
Light Meals

kiyosuku	kiosk	キヨスク
jun kissa	café	純喫茶
or *kissa ten*		喫茶店
keishoku kissa	tea house serving light meals	軽食喫茶

FOOD

roten	stand serving light Japanese-style meals	露店
sukiya	Japanese tea house	数寄屋
yatai	food stall	屋台
or *baiten*		売店

Bars

bā	(Western-style) bar	バー
izakaya	pub	居酒屋
kara oke	karaoke bar	カラオケ
kurabu	nightclub	クラブ
kyabarē	cabaret	キャバレー
nomiya	traditional Japanese bar	飲み屋
sunakku	licensed snack bar	スナック

Restaurants

chūka	Chinese restaurant	中華
or *chūka ryōri ten*		中華料理店
kappō	quality Japanese restaurant	割烹
or *ryōtei*		料亭
resutoran	restaurant	レストラン
ryōri ya	Japanese restaurant	料理屋
shokudō	cafeteria	食堂
soba ya	noodle shop	蕎麦屋
sushiya	sushi bar	寿司屋
tachi gui	fast-food stand	立食い

Cuisines

The word *ryōri* refers to a particular cuisine:

Chinese food	*chūgoku ryōri*	中国料理
Shanghai cuisine	*shanhai ryōri*	上海料理

vegetarian food	*shōjin ryōri*	精進料理
Japanese dishes	*nihon ryōri*	日本料理
	or *wa-shoku*	和食
Western dishes	*yō-shoku*	洋食

Japanese Dishes
Cooked in a Pot   *Nabe-Mono*   鍋物

oden　　　　　お田

　fishpaste cake (*chikuwa*), beancurd, cuttlefish, rolls of kelp
　(*kombu*), arum root paste *(kon nyaku)* and vegetables in fish
　broth

shabu shabu　　しゃぶしゃぶ

　various kinds of meat and vegetables simmered in broth

suki yaki　　　すき焼き

　beef, arum root gelatin noodles (*shirataki*), beancurd and
　vegetables, grilled on an iron pan and served with raw egg

yose nabe　　　寄せ鍋

　thick soup with seasonal ingredients

yu dōfu　　　　湯豆腐

　beancurd

Grilled & Fried   *Yaki-Mono*   焼き物

ishi yaki　　　石焼き

　broiled on a hot stone

kaba yaki　　　蒲焼き

　charcoal-broiled eel

kushi yaki　　　串焼き

　on skewers

robata yaki　　炉端焼き

　charcoal grilled

FOOD

shio yaki　　　　　　塩焼き
　fish and prawns with salt
teppan yaki　　　　　鉄板焼き
　beef and vegetables on an iron plate
teri yaki　　　　　　照焼き
　salty-sweet roast meat
tsubo yaki　　　　　壺焼き
　shellfish grilled in its own shell
yaki niku　　　　　　焼き肉
　pork
yaki tori　　　　　　焼き鳥
　chicken
yaki zakana　　　　　焼き魚
　fish

Japanese-Style Salads　　　*Ae-Mono*　　　和え物

These generally consist of seafood and vegetables, dressed with
vinegar, *miso* (bean paste) and sesame seeds.

goma ae　　　　　　胡麻和え
　vegetables (often spinach) with sesame seeds
komochi kombu　　　子持ち昆布
　caviar and kelp
nuta　　　　　　　　ぬた
　fish
sarada　　　　　　　サラダ
　salad
su dako　　　　　　酢蛸(すだこ)
　sliced octopus
wakamesu　　　　　わかめ酢
　seaweed

Pickled & Salted ***Tsuke-Mono*** 漬け物

ikura イクラ
  red caviar
karasumi からすみ
  mullet roe
miso zuke 味噌漬け
  pickles with bean paste *miso*
nara zuke 奈良漬け
  Nara-style pickled cucumber
shinkō 新香
  vegetables
takuan 沢庵
  radish
tarako 鱈子(たらこ)
  cod roe
ume boshi 梅干し
  plum

Soup ***Shiru-Mono*** 汁物
  or *Sui-Mono* 吸い物

dobin mushi 土瓶蒸し
  clear seafood soup
matsu take 松茸
  clear soup with pine mushrooms
miso shiru 味噌汁
  bean paste soup with beancurd, leek, seaweed, meats or
  seafood
nori sui 海苔吸い
  clear seaweed soup
sumashi 澄まし
  clear soup with seafood and vegetables

tai sui or *ushiojiru*　　鯛吸い/潮汁
　　clear soup with red snapper

Sushi　　　　　　　寿司

Sushi is generally raw seafood arranged on vinegared rice and Japanese horseradish, *wasabi*. Sometimes it is rolled in a thin sheet of dried *nori*, a type of seaweed, and then sliced.

chirashi　　　　　　チラシ
　　assorted fish and vegetables
futo maki　　　　　太巻き
　　large nori roll
gomoku zushi　　　五目寿司
　　variety of different types
ikura　　　　　　　イクラ
　　with caviar
inari　　　　　　　いなり
　　wrapped in fried seasoned beancurd
kappa　　　　　　　かっぱ
　　cucumber rolled in nori
maki zushi　　　　巻き寿司
　　rolled in nori
musubi　　　　　　結び
　　rice ball filled with salted plum or other ingredients
nigiri　　　　　　　にぎり
　　filled with pickles or salted fish and wrapped in nori
nori maki　　　　　海苔巻き
　　rolled in nori
tekka　　　　　　　鉄火
　　fish rolled in nori
temaki　　　　　　手巻き
　　special handmade nori roll

FOOD

Sashimi 刺し身

This is sliced raw meat or seafood, served with soy sauce and *wasabi*.

ike zukuri or *o-tsukuri* 生作り/お作り
  lobster, calamari or fish, sliced while still alive and reassembled in its former shape
... arai ...洗い
  fish
aji tataki 鰺たたき
  yellowtail, *aji*
basashi 馬刺し
  horse
gyūniku tataki 牛肉たたき
  beef
ise-ebi no sashimi 伊勢エビの刺し身
  lobster
katsuo tataki 鰹たたき
  pounded bonito

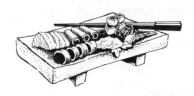

FOOD

Rice Dishes　　　　　　　　*Gohan-Mono*　　　御飯物

hayashi raisu　　　ハヤシ・ライス
  rice with meat and vegetables
kama meshi　　　釜飯
  rice in a pot
karē raisu　　　カレー・ライス
  rice with Japanese-style curry
kayu　　　粥(かゆ)
  rice porridge
ocha zuke　　　お茶漬け
  tea-flavoured rice with salted fish, pickles and shredded seaweed
pirafu　　　ピラフ
  Western-style pilaf
raisu or *gohan*　　　ライス/御飯
  plain rice
yaki meshi or *chāhan*　　焼き飯/チャーハン
  fried rice
yu zuke　　　湯付け
  rice with soup

Domburi　　　丼

This is rice with a topping of meat, vegetables or seafood. The most common types are:

chūka don　　　中華丼
  Chinese-style combination
gyū don　　　牛丼
  beef
kani tama　　　カニ玉
  crab meat and egg

katsu don カツ丼
  pork cutlet
oyako don 親子丼
  chicken and egg
ten don 天丼
  prawns in batter
unajū 鰻重
  broiled eel

Noodle Dishes   *Men-Rui*   麺類

cha soba 茶蕎麦
  tea-flavoured wheat noodles
chikara udon 力うどん
  noodles with rice-cake
gomoku soba 五目蕎麦
  noodles with assorted meats and vegetables
hiyashi soba 冷やし蕎麦
  cold noodles
kishimen きし麺
  Nagoya-style flat noodles
miso rāmen 味噌ラーメン
  noodles with miso
mori soba もり蕎麦
  cold noodles in fish broth with spring onions and *wasabi*
niku namban 肉南蛮
  noodles with meat and spring onions
rāmen ラーメン
  Chinese-style noodles
Sapporo rāmen 札幌ラーメン
  Sapporo-style noodles

FOOD

soba   蕎麦
  buckwheat noodles
udon   うどん
  thick wheat noodles
yaki soba or *chā men* 焼きそば/チャーメン
  fried noodles
zaru soba   ざる蕎麦
  mori soba noodles with sliced seaweed

Common toppings served with either *udon* or *soba* noodles are:

kake   かけ
  spring onion
kitsune   きつね
  fried seasoned beancurd
tempura   天ぷら
  vegetables and/or seafood in batter
tsukimi   月見
  egg

Deep-Fried Dishes   *Age-Mono*   揚げ物

abura age   油揚げ
  beancurd
kaki furai   カキ・フライ
  oysters
sakana no kara age   魚の空揚げ
  fish
tatsuta age   竜田揚げ
  marinated chicken
tempura   天ぷら
  vegetables and/or seafood in batter

ton katsu   トンカツ
  pork in breadcrumbs
wakatori kara age   若鳥空揚げ
  chicken

Steamed Dishes   *Mushi-Mono*   蒸し物

chawan mushi   茶碗蒸し
  chicken, vegetables and egg
komori mushi   こもり蒸し
  meat with mushrooms

Food for Special Occasions

ama guri   甘栗
  baked sweet chestnuts
ika yaki   イカ焼き
  grilled squid
mizu ame   水飴
  millet jelly
ningyō yaki   人形焼き
  sweet cake shaped like a doll
okonomi yaki   お好み焼き
  fried cabbage pancake
tako yaki   蛸(タコ)焼き
  octopus pancake
wata gashi   棉菓子
  fairy floss
yaki imo   焼きイモ
  baked sweet potato

FOOD

Soybean Dishes

nattō　　　　　　　納豆
　　fermented soybeans
agedashi dōfu　　　揚出し豆腐
　　deep-fried beancurd in broth
yakko　　　　　　　やっこ
　　cold beancurd with ginger

Banquet Cuisine

Banquets play an important role in Japanese life as guests are usually entertained at a restaurant rather than at home. The staple drink when eating out is *sake* (rice wine). Banquets generally begin with appetisers and then have an odd number of courses: three, five or seven. Courses are always presented with great artistry on lacquered trays along with the *sake*. At the end of the meal, *soba*, soup and rice with pickles are served.

Sea bream, *tai*, is always served as the main dish at a wedding or any other important occasion, as the word *tai* sounds like 'congratulations' in Japanese.

Breakfast

A Japanese-style breakfast will consist of savoury items such as pickles, soup, rice, *nori*, fermented soybeans, raw eggs and salted fish.

egg	*tamago*	玉子
fermented soybeans	*nattō*	納豆
fried fish	*yaki zakana*	焼き魚
pickles	*tsuke mono*	漬け物
	or *o-shinkō*	お新香
rice	*go han*	御飯
salad	*sarada*	サラダ
salted fish	*shio zakana*	塩魚

Western Breakfast

bacon	*bēkon*	ベーコン
boiled egg	*yude tamago*	ゆで玉子
bread	*pan*	パン
coffee	*kōhī*	コーヒー
fried egg	*medama yaki*	目玉焼き
ham	*hamu*	ハム
jam	*jamu*	ジャム
juice	*jūsu*	ジュース
milk	*miruku*	ミルク
sandwich	*sandoicchi*	サンドイッチ
sausage	*sōsēji*	ソーセージ
tea	*kōcha*	紅茶
toast	*tōsuto*	トースト

Meat & Poultry

beef	*gyū niku*	牛肉
chicken	*chikin*	チキン
duck	*kamo*	鴨
ham	*hamu*	ハム
meat	*niku*	肉
minced meat	*hiki niku*	挽き肉
mutton	*maton*	マトン
pork	*buta niku*	豚肉
sausage	*sōsēji*	ソーセージ
spareribs	*hone tsuki*	骨付き
tongue	*tan*	タン
turkey	*shichimen chō*	七面鳥

FOOD

Seafood

Japanese cuisine is centred around seafood. It is sometimes so fresh that the eyes and tail are said to be moving when it's served! Traditionally, Japanese have valued seafood caught just off-shore, but now, because of pollution and overwhelming demand, imports are growing.

abalone	*awabi*	鮑(アワビ)
bonito	*katsuo*	鰹(カツオ)
calamari	*yari ika*	槍烏賊(やりイカ)
clam	*hamaguri*	蛤(はまぐり)
cod	*tara*	鱈(たら)
crab	*kani*	蟹(カニ)
cuttlefish	*ika*	烏賊(イカ)
eel	*unagi*	鰻
fish cake	*kamaboko*	蒲鉾(かまぼこ)
fish	*sakana*	魚

FOOD

flounder	*karei*	鰈(カレイ)
herring	*nishin*	ニシン
jellyfish	*kurage*	くらげ
kingfish	*buri*	鰤(ブリ)
	or *hamachi*	はまち
lobster	*ise ebi*	伊勢エビ
	or *robusutā*	ロブスター
mackerel	*saba*	鯖(サバ)
mullet	*bora*	鯔(ぼら)
mussel	*mūru kai*	ムール貝
octopus	*tako*	蛸(タコ)
oyster	*kaki*	牡蠣(カキ)
perch	*suzuki*	鱸(スズキ)
prawn	*kuruma ebi*	車エビ
rainbow trout	*niji masu*	虹鱒
salmon	*sake*	鮭
salted fish	*shio zakana*	塩魚
sardine	*iwashi*	鰯(イワシ)
scallop	*hotate gai*	帆立貝
sea cucumber	*namako*	なまこ
shark's fin	*fukahire*	ふかひれ
shrimp	*shiba ebi*	芝エビ
snapper	*madai*	眞鯛
sole	*hirame*	平目(ひらめ)
squid	*ika*	烏賊(イカ)
trevally	*shima aji*	しまあじ
trout	*masu*	鱒(ます)
tuna	*maguro*	鮪(マグロ)
tuna berry	*toro*	とろ
whiting	*kisu*	キス
yellowtail	*aji*	鯵
	or *buri*	鰤(ブリ)

Vegetables

asparagus	*asuparagasu*	アスパラガス
bamboo shoots	*take no ko*	筍(タケノコ)
bean sprouts	*moyashi*	もやし
beancurd (tofu)	*tōfu*	豆腐
beans	*mame*	豆
beet	*aka kabu*	赤かぶ
broccoli	*burokkorī*	ブロッコリー
cabbage	*kyabetsu*	キャベツ
capsicum	*pīman*	ピーマン
carrot	*ninjin*	人参
cauliflower	*karifurawā*	カリフラワー
celery	*serori*	セロリ
Chinese cabbage	*hakusai*	白菜
corn	*tōmorokoshi*	とうもろこし
cucumber	*kyūri*	胡瓜(キューリ)
dried gourd	*kampyō*	干瓢
dried mushroom	*shiitake*	椎茸
eggplant	*nasu*	茄
gourd	*hyōtan*	瓢箪(ひょうたん)
green peas	*gurīn pīsu*	グリーン・ピース
green soybeans	*eda mame*	枝豆
Japanese mushroom	*matsutake*	松茸
kelp	*kombu*	昆布
leek	*naganegi*	長葱
	or *nira*	韮
lettuce	*retasu*	レタス
melon	*meron*	メロン
mushroom	*kinoko*	きのこ
	or *masshurūmu*	マッシュルーム
onion	*tamanegi*	玉葱

parsley	*paseri*	パセリ
pine mushroom	*matsu take*	松茸
potato	*jaga imo*	じゃが芋
pumpkin	*kabocha*	南瓜（カボチャ）
(white) radish	*daikon*	大根
seaweed	*wakame*	わかめ
(dried) seaweed	*nori*	海苔
soybean	*daizu*	大豆
spinach	*hōrensō*	ほうれん草
spring onion	*negi*	葱
sweet potato	*imo*	芋
taro	*satsuma imo*	薩摩芋
tomato	*tomato*	トマト
turnip	*kabu*	かぶ
vegetable	*yasai*	野菜

Fruit

apple	*ringo*	リンゴ
apricot	*anzu*	杏
cherry	*sakurambo*	さくらんぼ
chestnut	*kuri*	栗
date	*natsume*	なつめ
fruit	*kudamono*	果物
	or *furūtsu*	フルーツ
grapefruit	*gurēpu furūtsu*	グレープ・フルーツ
honeydew melon	*meron*	メロン
lemon	*remon*	レモン
mandarin	*mikan*	蜜柑
nectarine	*nekutarin*	ネクタリン
nut	*nattsu*	ナッツ

orange	*orenji*	オレンジ
peach	*momo*	桃
peanut	*pīnattsu*	ピーナッツ
pear	*nashi*	梨
pineapple	*painappuru*	パイナップル
plum	*sumomo*	李(すもも)
raisin	*rēzun*	レーズン
strawberry	*ichigo*	苺
tomato	*tomato*	トマト
walnut	*kurumi*	胡桃
watermelon	*suika*	西瓜

Dairy products

butter	*batā*	バター
cheese	*chīzu*	チーズ
cream	*kurīmu*	クリーム
ice cream	*aisu kurīmu*	アイス・クリーム
margarine	*māgarin*	マーガリン
milk	*gyūnyū*	牛乳
	or *miruku*	ミルク
milk powder	*kona miruku*	粉ミルク
milk shake	*miruku sēki*	ミルク・セーキ
skim milk	*sukimu miruku*	スキム・ミルク
yoghurt	*yōguruto*	ヨーグルト

Cakes & Sweets

Japanese cakes and sweets feature such ingredients as rice, wheat flour, red beans, agar-agar, sugar, egg, sesame seeds, and even seaweed and tea powder. They are divided into two major types: *nama-gashi*, which are fresh and moist, and *hi-gashi*, which are generally baked. Japanese traditionally enjoy sweets with green tea, and sweets are central to the famous Japanese tea ceremony.

At New Year Japanese eat *mochi*, a sticky rice cake, and offer *kakami mochi*, a special pair of rice cakes, to the gods.

FOOD

daifuku mochi　　　大福餅
  dumpling stuffed with red bean paste
kuri manjū　　　栗饅頭
  bun with chestnut jam
manjū　　　饅頭
  bun with red bean paste
mizu yōkan　　　水羊羹
  soft sweet bean jelly
mochi　　　餅
  rice cake
sakura-mochi　　　桜餅
  sticky rice ball with red bean paste
sasadango　　　笹団子
  steamed sticky rice dumpling stuffed with red bean paste and
  wrapped in bamboo leaves
sembei　　　煎餅
  rice crackers
yōkan　　　羊羹
  red bean jelly

Seasonings & Condiments

bean paste	*miso*	味噌
chilli	*tōgarashi*	唐辛子
curry	*karē*	カレー
garlic	*ninniku*	大蒜(ニンニク)
ginger	*shōga*	生姜(ショウガ)
grated radish	*daikon oroshi*	大根おろし
honey	*hachimitsu*	蜂蜜
(green) horseradish	*wasabi*	わさび
Japanese pepper	*sanshō*	山椒
ketchup	*kechappu*	ケチャップ
mayonnaise	*mayonēzu*	マヨネーズ

mint	*hakka*	薄荷
MSG	*aji no moto*	味の素
mustard	*karashi*	芥子(からし)
oil	*abura*	油
pepper	*koshō*	胡椒
pepper & salt mixture	*shio koshō*	塩胡椒
salt	*shio*	塩
sauce	*sōsu*	ソース
sesame oil	*goma abura*	胡麻油
sesame seeds	*goma*	胡麻
soy sauce	*shōyu*	醤油
sugar	*satō*	砂糖
tabasco	*tabasuko*	タバスコ
tomato sauce	*tomato sōsu*	トマト・ソース
vinegar	*osu*	お酢
wine (rice)	*sake*	酒

Some uniquely Japanese seasonings:

dashi	fish broth	出し
katsuobushi	dried bonito shavings	鰹節
mirin	sweet rice wine used in cooking	味醂(みりん)
miso	bean paste	味噌
ponzu	sauce for rice, vegetables, beancurd and fish	ポンズ
tare	sauce used in *teri yaki*, *suki yaki* and *yaki niku*	垂れ

tsuyu	all-purpose soup base	汁/液
ume boshi	dried salted plum	梅干し

What seasonings are in this?
nan no kōshinryō ga haitte i masu ka? 何の香辛料が 入っていますか?

Is there any ... in this?
... wa haitte i masu ka? ...は 入っていますか?

Please don't add any ...
... wa irenai de kudasai ...は 入れないで下さい

Please add some ...
... wa irete kudasai ...は 入れて下さい

I like ... (very much).
... wa (dai) suki desu ...は (大)好きです

Preferences

Do you like ... food?	*... mono wa o-suki desu ka?*	...物は お好き ですか?
I like ... food.	*watashi wa ... mono ga suki desu*	私は...物が 好きです
I don't like ... food.	*... mono wa amari suki dewa ari masen*	...物は あまり 好きではありません
This/That is ...	*(kore)/(sore) wa ... desu*	(これ)/(それ)は ...です
bitter	*nigai*	苦い
cold	*tsumetai*	冷たい
crispy	*paripari shita*	パリパリした
delicious	*oishii*	美味しい
	or *umai*	旨い

dry (wine)	*kara kuchi*	辛口
fishy	*nama gusai*	生臭い
fresh	*shinsen (na)*	新鮮（な）
hot (spicy)	*karai*	辛い
hot (temperature)	*atsui*	熱い
light (wine)	*ama kuchi*	甘口
nice	*ii*	いい
	or *yoi*	よい
not nice	*mazui*	まずい
oily	*aburakkoi*	油っこい
plain	*assari shita*	あっさりした
raw	*nama*	生
salty	*shio karai*	塩辛い
sour	*suppai*	酸っぱい
sweet	*amai*	甘い
tart	*shibui*	渋い
tender	*yawarakai*	軟らかい
tough	*katai*	堅い
warm	*atatakai*	暖かい

FOOD

Drinks

I'd like a (lemon squash).
  (remon sukasshu) o kudasai   （レモン・スカッシュ）を下さい
I'd like (two glasses of) beer.
  bīru o (ni hai) kudasai   ビールを（２杯）下さい

apple juice	*ringo jūsu*	リンゴ・ジュース
beer	*bīru*	ビール
beverage	*nomimono*	飲み物
brandy	*burandē*	ブランデー
champagne	*shampen*	シャンペン

cider	*saidā*	サイダー
Coca Cola	*koka kōra*	コカ・コーラ
cognac	*konyakku*	コニャック
cola	*kōra*	コーラ
cold water	*o-mizu*	お水
distilled wine	*shōchū*	焼酎
draft beer	*nama bīru*	生ビール
(fresh) fruit juice	*(nama) jūsu*	(生)ジュース
gin	*jin*	ジン
hot water	*o-yu*	お湯
iced coffee	*aisu kōhī*	アイス・コーヒー
iced tea	*aisu tī*	アイス・ティー
iced water	*o-hiya*	お冷や
lemonade	*remonēdo*	レモネード
milk	*miruku*	ミルク
	or *gyūnyū*	牛乳
mineral water	*mineraru uōtā*	ミネラル・ウォーター
orange juice	*orenji jūsu*	オレンジ・ジュース
plum wine	*ume shu*	梅酒
sake	*o-sake*	お酒
	or *nihon shu*	日本酒
soda water	*sōda sui*	ソーダ水
spiced sake	*toso*	屠蘇(とそ)
squash	*sukasshu*	スカッシュ
sweet wine	*ama zake*	甘酒
tomato juice	*tomato jūsu*	トマト・ジュース
tonic	*tonikku*	トニック
whisky	*uisukī*	ウイスキー
whisky with water	*mizu wari*	水割り
(Western) wine	*wain*	ワイン

Some Useful Words

alcoholic	*arukōru*	アルコール
(two) bottles	*(ni) hon*	(2)本
(two) cups	*(ni) hai*	(2)杯
Cheers!	*kampai!*	乾杯！
glass	*gurasu*	グラス
sake bottle	*tokkuri*	徳利(とっくり)
wine glass	*wain gurasu*	ワイン・グラス
wine list	*wain risuto*	ワイン・リスト

Tea

Bancha tea	*ban cha*	番茶
Chinese tea	*chūgoku cha*	中国茶
fresh tea	*shin cha*	新茶
green tea	*ryoku cha*	緑茶
Gyokuro tea	*gyokuro*	玉露
Japanese tea	*nihon cha*	日本茶
powdered green tea	*maccha*	抹茶
Sencha tea	*sen cha*	煎茶
tea	*cha*	茶
	or *o-cha*	お茶
tea powder	*kona cha*	粉茶
tea with milk	*miruku tī*	ミルク・ティー
Western tea	*kōcha*	紅茶
wheat tea	*mugi cha*	麦茶
Wulong tea	*ūron cha*	烏龍(ウーロン)茶

Other Hot Drinks

black coffee	*burakku*	ブラック
cocoa	*kokoa*	ココア
coffee	*kōhī*	コーヒー

hot coffee	*hotto*	ホット
	or *hotto kōhī*	ホット・コーヒー
hot Japanese wine	*atsu kan*	熱燗
hot Shaoxing wine	*shōkōshu*	紹興酒
hot water	*o-yu*	お湯
instant coffee	*insutanto kōhī*	インスタント・コーヒー
whisky with hot water	*o-yu wari*	お湯割り

FOOD

Cutlery & Accessories

ashtray	*haizara*	灰皿
bottle-opener	*sen neki*	栓抜き
bowl	*hachi*	鉢
	or *wan*	椀
bowl for rice	*chawan*	茶碗
chopsticks	*hashi*	箸
chopsticks (disposable)	*wari bashi*	割り箸
fork	*fōku*	フォーク
glass	*gurasu*	グラス
napkin	*napukin*	ナプキン
sake cup	*saka zuki*	杯
toothpick	*tsuma yōji*	爪楊枝

Shopping

Many shoppers are attracted by the quality and range of goods available in Japan, even though prices can be a bit higher than in other countries of the region.

I'd like this/that.
   (kore)/(sore) o o-negai shimasu   (これ)/(それ)をお願いします

I'm just looking.
   mite iru dake desu   見ているだけです

Please show me this/that.
   (kore)/(sore) o misete kudasai   (これ)/(それ)を見せて下さい

How much does this/that cost?
   (kore)/(sore) wa ikura desu ka?   (これ)/(それ)は幾らですか？

(That is) expensive.
   (sore wa) takai desu   (それは)高いです

(This is) cheap.
   (kore wa) yasui desu   (これは)安いです

Where do I pay?
   shiharai wa dochira desu ka?   支払いは どちらですか？

Could you wrap it for me?
   tsutsunde kure masen ka?   包んでくれませんか？

Can I have a receipt?
   ryōshūsho o kudasai masen ka?   領収書を下さいませんか？

Shops

Japanese commonly refer to a shop using the name of the product sold there plus *ya*. For example, *hana* means flower, and so florist is *hana ya*.

Where is ...?	*... wa dochira desu ka?*	...はどちらですか？
I am looking for (a/an) ...	*... o sagashite imasu ga*	...を探していますが
antique shop	*kottō ya*	骨董屋
baker	*pan ya*	パン屋
bank	*ginkō*	銀行
barber	*toko ya*	床屋

bookshop	*hon ya*	本屋
	or *sho ten*	書店
boutique	*butikku*	ブティック
butcher	*niku ya*	肉屋
cake shop	*kēki ya*	ケーキ屋
camera shop	*shashin ya*	写真屋
china shop	*setomono ya*	瀬戸物屋
confectionery	*okashi ya*	お菓子屋
department store	*depāto*	デパート
	or *hyakka ten*	百貨店
dress shop	*yōfuku ya*	洋服屋
dutyfree shop	*menzei ten*	免税店
electrical shop	*denki ya*	電気屋

fish shop	*sakana ya*	魚屋
florist	*hana ya*	花屋
folk art shop	*mingei hin ten*	民芸品店
fruit shop	*kudamono ya*	果物屋
greengrocer	*shokuryōhin ten*	食料品店
grocery	*zakka ya*	雑貨屋
hairdresser	*biyōin*	美容院
handicraft shop	*shukōgeihin ten*	手工芸品店
jeweller	*hōseki ten*	宝石店
kiosk	*bai ten*	売店
	or *kiyosuku*	キヨスク
laundry	*sentaku ya*	洗濯屋
market	*ichiba*	市場
money exchange office	*ryōgae jo*	両替所
musical instrument shop	*gakki ten*	楽器店
pawnbroker	*shichi ya*	質屋
pharmacy	*yakkyoku*	薬局
	or *kusuri ya*	薬屋
shoe shop	*kutsu ya*	靴屋
shop	*mise*	店
souvenir shop	*miyage mono ya*	土産物屋
store	*sutoā*	ストア
supermarket	*sūpā*	スーパー
	or *sūpā māketto*	スーパー・マーケット
tailor	*yōfuku ya*	洋服屋
	or *shitate ya*	仕立て屋
toy shop	*omocha ya*	玩具屋
trading firm	*bōeki gaisha*	貿易会社
vegetable shop	*yao ya*	八百屋
wine shop	*saka ya*	酒屋

Bargain Sales

Generally you shouldn't try to bargain in a shop or department store, except during a designated bargain sale, called a *yasu uri* or *uri dashi*.

It's expensive.
sorewa takai desu それは高いです

It's too expensive.
sorewa takasugi masu それは高すぎます

Could you reduce the price?
makete kudasai まけて下さい

Do you give a discount?
waribiki shite kure masen ka? 割引してくれませんか？

Can you give a 10%/20% discount?
(ichi)/(ni) waribiki shite kure masen ka? (一)/(二)割引して くれませんか？

Souvenirs

bathrobe	*yukata*	浴衣
chinaware	*setomono*	瀬戸物
clock	*tokei*	時計
cloisonné	*shippō yaki*	七宝焼き
curios	*kottō hin*	骨董品
doll	*ningyō*	人形
fan (folding)	*sensu*	扇子
fan (round)	*uchiwa*	団扇
food	*shokuryōhin*	食料品
furniture	*kagu*	家具
handbag	*hando baggu*	ハンド・バッグ
handicraft	*shukōgeihin*	手工芸品
helmet	*kabuto*	兜

jewellery	*hōseki*	宝石
kimono	*kimono*	着物
lacquerware	*shikki*	漆器
leatherwork	*kawa seihin*	革製品
musical instrument	*gakki*	楽器
necklace	*nekkuresu*	ネックレス
painting (Japanese)	*nihon ga*	日本画
painting (oil)	*abura e*	油絵
painting (Western)	*yō ga*	洋画
painting/picture	*e*	絵
paper (Japanese)	*washi*	和紙
paper cuttings	*kiri kami*	切り紙
pearl	*shinju*	真珠
personal seal	*inkan*	印鑑
postcard	*e hagaki*	絵葉書き
pottery	*tōki*	陶器
sculpture	*chōkoku*	彫刻
souvenir	*o-miyage*	お土産
sword	*katana*	刀
toy	*omocha*	玩具
umbrella	*kasa*	傘

SHOPPING

| woodblock print | *mokuhan ga* | 木版画 |
| woodblock print (traditional) | *ukiyo e* | 浮世絵 |

Electrical Equipment

In Japan you'll find the most up-to-date electrical goods.

calculator	*keisanki*	計算機
cassette recorder	*kasetto tēpu rekōda*	カセット・テープ レコーダ
cassette tape	*kasetto tēpu*	カセット・テープ
computer	*kompyūtā*	コンピューター
cord	*kōdo*	コード
floppy disk	*furoppī disuku*	フロッピー・ディスク
microphone	*maiku*	マイク
microwave oven	*denshi renji*	電子レンジ
plug	*sashikomi* or *puragu*	差込み プラグ
program	*puroguramu*	プログラム
radio	*rajio*	ラジオ
record	*rekōdo*	レコード
TV	*terebi*	テレビ
video camera	*bideo kamera*	ビデオ・カメラ
video laser disk	*rēzā disuku*	レーザー・ディスク
video tape	*bideo tēpu*	ビデオ・テープ
virus	*uīrusu*	ウィルス
voltage	*den atsu*	電圧
word processor	*wāpuro*	ワープロ

SHOPPING

Photography

I'd like a ...	... o kudasai	...を下さい
24/36 exposure colour film	(nijūyon)/(san-jūroku) mai dori karā firumu	(24)/(36)枚撮り カラー・フィルム
B&W film	shiro kuro firumu	白黒フィルム
cartridge	kātorijji	カートリッジ
colour slide film	karā suraido firumu	カラー・スラード フィルム
disk film	disuku firumu	ディスク・フィルム
high speed film	kōkando firumu	高感度フィルム
Super 8	sūpā eito	スーパー 8

I'd like this developed ...	... genzō o o-negai shi masu	...現像を お願いします
with a gloss finish	kōtaku shiage de	光沢仕上げで
with a matt finish	matto shiage de or tsuya keshi no	マット仕上げで つや消しの

How many ... will it take?	... kurai kakari masu ka?	...くらい かかりますか?
minutes	nan bun	何分
hours	nan jikan	何時間
days	nan nichi	何日

How much (for one print)?
(ichi mai) ikura desu ka?　　　(一枚)幾らですか?

battery	denchi	電池
camera	kamera	カメラ

colour	*karā*	カラー
develop	*genzō shimasu*	現像します
enlargement	*hikinobashi*	引伸ばし
extra print	*yakimashi*	焼増し
film	*firumu*	フィルム
flash	*furasshu*	フラッシュ
lens	*renzu*	レンズ
negatives	*nega*	ネガ
passport photo	*pasupōto yō shashin*	パスポート用写真
photo	*shashin*	写真
print	*purinto*	プリント
size	*saizu*	サイズ
slide	*suraido*	スライド
timer	*taimā*	タイマー
tripod	*sankyaku*	三脚
video camera	*bideo kamera*	ビデオ・カメラ

Clothing

belt	*beruto*	ベルト
boots	*naga gutsu*	長靴
	or *būtsu*	ブーツ
clothing	*irui*	衣類
coat	*uwagi*	上着
dress	*doresu*	ドレス
footwear	*hakimono*	履物
formal dress	*fōmaru doresu*	フォーマル・ドレス
	or *seisō*	正装
handerchief	*hankachi*	ハンカチ
hat	*bōshi*	帽子
jacket	*jaketto*	ジャケット
Japanese-style	*wa fuku*	和服

clothing	or *go fuku*	呉服
jeans	*jīpan*	ジーパン
	or *jīnzu*	ジーンズ
jumper	*jampā*	ジャンパー
nightgown	*nemaki*	寝巻き
overcoat	*ōbā kōto*	オーバー・コート
pyjamas	*pajama*	パジャマ
raincoat	*rein kōto*	レイン・コート
sandals	*sandaru*	サンダル
scarf	*sukāfu*	スカーフ
shirt	*shatsu*	シャツ
shoelaces	*kutsu himo*	靴ひも
shoes	*kutsu*	靴
shorts	*han zubon*	半ズボン
skirt	*sukāto*	スカート
slippers	*surippa*	スリッパ
socks	*kutsu shita*	靴下
stockings	*sutokkingu*	ストッキング
sweater	*sētā*	セーター
swimsuit	*mizugi*	水着
T-shirt	*T-shatsu*	Ｔーシャツ
tie	*nekutai*	ネクタイ
trousers	*zubon*	ズボン
underwear	*shitagi*	下着
	or *hadagi*	肌着
Western-style clothing	*yō fuku*	洋服

SHOPPING

Traditional Japanese Clothing

geta 下駄
    wooden clogs

hakama 袴(はかま)
  wide trousers
juban 襦袢(じゅばん)
  underwear
kimono 着物
  traditional and formal robe, often made from silk
nemaki 寝巻き
  Japanese-style pyjamas
obi 帯
  broad sash for a kimono
tabi 足袋
  socks worn with a kimono
yukata 浴衣
  cotton robe, a less formal version of a kimono
zōri 草履
  sandals

Materials

cashmere	*kashimia*	カシミア
cotton	*men*	綿
fabric	*kiji*	生地
leather	*kawa*	革
linen	*asa*	麻
nylon	*nairon*	ナイロン
silk	*kinu*	絹
thread	*ito*	糸
wool	*ūru*	ウール

Colours

light ...	*asai* ...	浅い
	or *usui* ...	薄い
dark ...	*koi* ...	濃い
	or *fukai* ...	深い
black	*kuro*	黒
black and white	*shiro kuro*	白黒
blue	*ao*	青
	or *kon*	紺
brown	*cha iro*	茶色
gold	*kin iro*	金色
green	*gurīn*	グリーン
	or *midori*	緑
grey	*hai iro*	灰色
	or *gurei*	グレイ
indigo	*ai iro*	藍色
light blue	*mizu iro*	水色
pink	*momo iro*	桃色
	or *sakura iro*	桜色
red	*aka*	赤

silver	*gin iro*	銀色
	or *shirubā*	シルバー
violet	*murasaki*	紫
white	*shiro*	白
yellow	*ki iro*	黄色

Descriptions

big	*ookii*	大きい
cheap	*yasui*	安い
expensive	*takai*	高い
fits well	*ai masu*	合います
good	*ii*	いい
	or *yoi*	よい
long	*nagai*	長い
loose	*yurui*	緩い
narrow	*semai*	狭い
pretty	*kirei na*	綺麗な
round	*marui*	丸い
short	*mijikai*	短い
small	*chiisai*	小さい
suits me/you	*niai masu*	似合います
tight	*kitsui*	きつい
wide	*hiroi*	広い
	or *ookii*	大きい

Books & Stationery

adhesive	*secchaku zai*	接着剤
ballpoint pen	*bōru pen*	ボール・ペン
book	*hon*	本
calculator	*keisanki*	計算機
calendar	*karendā*	カレンダー

SHOPPING

correction fluid	*shūseieki*	修正液
dictionary	*jisho*	辞書
eraser	*keshi gomu*	消しゴム
envelope	*fūtō*	封筒
ink	*inki*	インキ
magazine	*zasshi*	雑誌
map	*chizu*	地図
newspaper	*shimbun*	新聞
newspaper in English	*eigo no shimbun*	英語の新聞
novel	*shōsetsu*	小説
paper	*kami*	紙
pencil	*empitsu*	鉛筆
rubber bands	*wa gomu*	輪ゴム
scissors	*hasami*	鋏み(はさみ)
typewriter	*taipu raitā*	タイプ・ライター
weekly magazine	*shūkanshi*	週刊誌
writing paper	*binsen*	便箋

Toiletries

baby powder	*bebī paudā*	ベビー・パウダー
baby's bottle	*ho nyū bin*	哺乳瓶
candle	*rōsoku*	蝋燭(ろうそく)
comb	*kushi*	くし
conditioner	*rinsu*	リンス
	or *kondishonā*	コンディショナー
condoms	*kondōmu*	コンドーム
cosmetics	*keshōhin*	化粧品
cream	*kurīmu*	クリーム
dental floss	*dentaru furosu*	デンタル・フロス
deodorant	*deodoranto*	デオドラント

drinking water	nomi mizu	飲み水
face powder	oshiroi	白粉
hairbrush	hea burashu	ヘア・ブラシュ
lipstick	kuchi beni	口紅
match	macchi	マッチ
mirror	kagami	鏡
nail clippers	tsume kiri	爪切り
razor blades	kamisori no ha	カミソリの刃
rouge	hoho beni	ほほ紅
shampoo	shampū	シャンプー
soap	sekken	石鹸
sunblock cream	hiyake dome kurīmu	日焼止めクリーム
talcum powder	bodi paudā	ボディ・パウダー
tampons	tampon	タンポン
tissues	tisshu	ティッシュ
toilet paper	toiretto pēpā	トイレット・ペーパー
toothbrush	haburashi	歯ブラシ
toothpaste	hamigaki	歯磨き
towel	taoru	タオル

Some Useful Words

buy (v)	kai masu	買います
cashier	kanjōsho	勘定所
	or kaikeijo	会計所
cheap	yasui	安い
counter	kauntā	カウンター
discount	waribiki	割引
expensive	takai	高い
half-price	hangaku	半額
GST	shōhi zei	消費税
information	annai jo	案内所

SHOPPING

list price	*teika*	定価
market price	*sōba*	相場
no discount	*waribiki nashi*	割引なし
not for sale	*hibaihin*	非売品
price	*nedan*	値段
	or *kakaku*	価格
receipt	*ryōshūsho*	領収書
	or *reshīto*	レシート
receptionist	*uketsuke kakari*	受付係り
register	*reji*	レジ
sold out	*urikire*	売切れ
special product	*meibutsu*	名物
today's special	*kyō no*	今日のお買得品
	o-kaidoku-hin	
trading area	*uriba*	売り場

Health

Japanese medicine combines both Eastern and Western medical practices, giving you a choice of traditional treatments (such as *shiatsu* and acupuncture) or the latest in medical technology. If you have any difficulties communicating, try writing your problem down, as most Japanese doctors can read medical English very well. Emergency medical facilities are commonly available at stations and information centres. First-aid kits are normally marked with a green cross.

It's worth taking out medical insurance as treatment in Japan is expensive!

I am sick.
guai ga warui desu　　　　　　具合が悪いです
My wife/husband is sick.
(tsuma)/(shujin) ga byōki desu　(妻)/(主人)が病気です
I am not feeling well.
kibun ga warui desu　　　　　　気分が悪いです
I need a doctor.
o-isha san ni mite morai　　　　お医者さんに
tai desu　　　　　　　　　　　　見てもらいたいです
I need a doctor who can speak English.
ei-go no dekiru o-isha san ga　　英語のできるお医者さんが
i masu ka?　　　　　　　　　　　いますか?
I need an English interpreter.
ei-go no tsūyaku ga i masu ka?　英語の通訳が いますか?
I need a female doctor.
joi san ga i masu ka?　　　　　　女医さんが いますか?

HEALTH

Please call a doctor to room ...
   ... gō shitsu ni o-isha san o yonde
   kudasai   ... 号室にお医者さんを
                           呼んで下さい

Please take me to a doctor.
   o-isha san ni tsurete
   itte kudasai   お医者さんに連れて
                           行って下さい

I have been injured.
   watashi wa kega o shite i masu   私は怪我をしています

I need an ambulance.
   kyūkyūsha o yonde kudasai   救急車を呼んで下さい

I have to go to the casualty ward
(emergency department).
   kyūkyūshitsu ni ikanakereba
   narimasen   救急室に行かなければ
                           なりません

I need first aid.
   ōkyū teate o shite kudasai   応急手当をして下さい

Where is the ...?   *... wa dochira desu ka?* ...はどちらですか？

casualty ward	*kyūkyūshitsu*	救急室
clinic	*shinryōjo*	診療室
	or *kurinikku*	クリニック
dentist	*ha-isha*	歯医者
doctor	*isha*	医者
hospital	*byōin*	病院
nurse (m)	*kango-shi*	看護士
nurse (f)	*kango-fu*	看護婦
pharmacy	*yakkyoku*	薬局
surgery	*shujutsu shitsu*	手術室

How long will it take to get better?
naoru made dono kurai kakari   治るまでどのくらい
masu ka?   かかりますか？

Questions

どうしましたか？	*dō shi mashita ka?*	What's wrong?
どこが痛いですか？	*doko ga itai desu ka?*	Where does it hurt?
気分はいかがですか？	*kibun wa ikaga desu ka?*	How are you feeling?
どこが痛みますか？	*doko ga itami masu ka?*	Do you feel any pain?
熱はありますか？	*netsu wa ari masu ka?*	Do you have a tempera-ture?
今までに大きな病気をした事がありますか？	*imma made ni ookina byōki o shita koto ga ari masu ka?*	What illnesses have you had in the past?
たばこは吸いますか？	*tabako wa suimasu ka?*	Do you smoke?
お酒は飲みますか？	*o-sake wa nomi masu ka?*	Do you drink?

Some Useful Words & Phrases

I ...
 watashi wa ...
 私は...

 have been bitten by an insect
 mushi ni sasare mashita
 虫に刺されました

can't move my ...	... o ugokase masen	...を動かせません
can't sleep	nemure masen	眠れません
have a heart condition	shin zō byō ga ari masu	心臓病があります
have no appetite	shoku yoku ga arimasen	食欲がありません
have not had my period for ... months	... ka getsu hodo seiri ga ari masen	...ヶ月ほど 生理がありません
am on the pill	piru o nonde i masu	ピルを飲んでいます
am pregnant	nin-shin shite i masu	妊娠しています
am vomiting	hakike ga shi masu	吐き気がします
feel lethargic	hidoku tsukarete i masu	ひどく疲れています

It's ...	koko ga ...	ここが...
bleeding	shukketsu shite i masu	出血しています
broken	orete i masu	折れています
bruised	nai shukketsu shite i masu	内出血しています
dislocated	dakkyū shite i masu	脱臼しています
sprained	nenza shite i masu	捻挫しています
swollen	harete i masu	腫れています

I have ...	watashi wa ...	私は...
altitude sickness	kōsho kyōfu shō desu	高所恐怖症です
appendicitis	mōchōen desu	盲腸炎です
arthritis	kansetsuen desu	関節炎です
asthma	zensoku desu	喘息です
a backache	yōtsū ga ari masu	腰痛があります
breathing trouble	kokyū konnan desu	呼吸困難です
a burn	yakedo shi mashita	火傷しました
cold sweats	hiya ase ga de masu	冷や汗が出ます
a cold	kaze o hiki mashita	風を引きました
constipation	bempi ni natte imasu	便秘になっています
a cough	seki ga de masu	咳が出ます
cramps	komura gaeri shi masu	こむら返りします
diabetes	tōnyōbyō desu	糖尿病です
diarrhoea	geri o shite imasu	下痢をしています
dizzy spells	memai ga shi masu	目眩がします
a duodenal ulcer	jūnishichō kaiyō desu	十二指腸潰瘍です
a fever	netsu ga ari masu	熱があります
food poisoning	shoku chūdoku desu	食中毒です
hay fever	kafun shō desu	花粉症です
a headache	zutsū ga shi masu	頭痛がします
hepatitis	kan en desu	肝炎です
high blood pressure	kōketsuatsu desu	高血圧です

indigestion	*shōka furyō desu*	消化不良です
influenza	*infuruenza desu*	インフルエンザです
insomnia	*fumin shō desu*	不眠症です
an itch	*kayui desu*	痒いです
lice	*shirami ga i masu*	虱がいます
low blood pressure	*teiketsuatsu desu*	低血圧です
malaria	*marariya desu*	マラリヤです
a migraine	*henzutsū desu*	偏頭痛です
a nervous breakdown	*shinkei suijaku desu*	弱衰衰弱です
no appetite	*shoku yoku fushin desu*	食欲不振です
a runny nose	*hana mizu ga de masu*	鼻水が出ます
seasickness	*funa yoi desu*	船酔いです
a sore throat	*nodo ga itai desu*	喉が痛いです
a stomachache	*fukutsū ga shi masu*	腹痛がします
a stomach ulcer	*ikaiyō desu*	胃潰瘍です
sunstroke	*nissha byō desu*	日射病です
tonsillitis	*hentōsen en desu*	扁桃腺炎です
a toothache	*ha ga itai desu*	歯が痛いです
travel sickness	*norimono yoi ga shi masu*	乗物酔がします
typhoid fever	*chifusu desu*	チフスです
an ulcer	*kaiyō ga ari masu*	潰瘍があります
a venereal disease	*seibyō desu*	性病です
been vomiting	*ōto ga ari masu*	嘔吐があります

Allergies

I'm allergic to ...	*watashi wa ...* *arerugī desu*	私は...アレルギーです
antibiotics	*kōsei busshitsu*	抗生物質
aspirin	*asupirin*	アスピリン
codeine	*kodein*	コデイン
dairy products	*nyūseihin*	乳製品
food colouring	*jinkō chakushoku* *ryō*	人工着色料
meat	*niku rui*	肉類
MSG	*aji no moto*	味の素
penicillin	*penishirin*	ペニシリン
pollen	*kafun*	花粉

I have a skin allergy.

watashi wa atopī arerugī desu	私はアトピー・アレルギーです

At the Pharmacy

In most cases, the doctor or clinic will provide prescribed medicines.

Japan produces its own range of pharmaceuticals, so it may be difficult to find the brand you use at home – bring prescribed drugs with you.

Can I please have ...	*sumi masen ga, ... o kudasai*	すみませんが、 ...を下さい
an analgesic	*chintsū zai*	鎮痛剤
aspirin	*asupirin*	アスピリン
a bandage	*hōtai*	包帯
Band-aids	*bando eido*	バンド・エイド
condoms	*kondōmu*	コンドーム

cotton buds	menbō	綿棒
cough medicine	seki dome	咳止め
a cup of water	o-mizu	お水
eye drops	me gusuri	目薬
insect repellent spray	mushi yoke supurē	虫除けスプレー
a laxative	ge zai	下剤
mercurochrome	aka chin	赤チン
pain killers	itami dome	痛み止め
the pill	piru	ピル
	or hinin yaku	避妊薬
sanitary napkins	seiri yō napukin	生理用ナプキン
sleeping pills	suimin yaku	睡眠薬
tablets for fever	genetsu zai	解熱剤
tampons	tampon	タンポン
a thermometer	taion kei	体温計

What You Might Hear

一日（4）回、一回（2）錠を飲んで下さい	ichi nichi (yon)-kai, ikkai (ni)-jō o nonde kudasai	Please take (two) tablets (four) times a day.
一日（2）回患部に塗って下さい	ichi nichi (ni)-kai kambu ni nutte kudasai	Apply to the affected area (two) times a day.
食（前）/（後）	shoku (zen)/(go)	before/after meals
就寝前	shūshin mae	before bedtime

tiger balm	*taigā bāmu*	タイガー・バーム
a tranquilliser	*chinsei zai*	鎮静剤
travel sickness pills	*yoi dome*	酔止め

Parts of the Body

ankle	*kurubushi*	踝(くるぶし)
appendix	*mōchō*	盲腸
arm	*ude*	腕
armpit	*waki no shita*	脇の下
back	*senaka*	背中
blood	*chi*	血
	or *ketsu eki*	血液
bone	*hone*	骨
brain	*nō*	脳
chest	*mune*	胸(むね)
chin	*ago*	顎(あご)
ear	*mimi*	耳
elbow	*hiji*	肘(ひじ)
eye	*me*	目
face	*kao*	顔
finger	*yubi*	指
fingernail	*tsume*	爪
foot	*ashi*	足
gall bladder	*tan nō*	胆嚢
gall stone	*tan seki*	胆石
hair	*kaminoke*	髪の毛
hand	*te*	手
head	*atama*	頭
heart	*shinzō*	心臓
leg	*ashi*	足

lung	*hai*	肺
mouth	*kuchi*	口
muscle	*kinniku*	筋肉
nerve	*shinkei*	神経
nose	*hana*	鼻
shoulder	*kata*	肩
skin	*hifu*	皮膚
spine	*sebone*	背骨
stomach	*i*	胃
teeth	*ha*	歯
throat	*nodo*	喉
tongue	*shita*	舌
tonsils	*hentōsen*	扁桃腺
urine	*nyō*	尿
vein	*jōmyaku*	静脈

At the Dentist

Is there a dentist here?
   ha-isha wa ari masu ka?   歯医者はありますか？
I don't want it extracted.
   ha o nuka naide kudasai   歯を抜かないで下さい
Please give me an anaesthetic.
   masui o kake te kudasai   麻酔をかけて下さい

decayed tooth	*mushi-ba*	虫歯
dentist	*ha-isha*	歯医者
denture	*ireba*	入れ歯
filling	*jūten*	充填
fluoride treatment	*fusso tofu*	弗素塗布（ふっそとふ）
jaw bone	*ago*	顎（あご）
milk teeth	*nyūshi*	乳歯

root	*haguki*	歯茎
tooth	*ha*	歯
toothache	*shitsū*	歯痛
	or *haita*	歯痛
wisdom tooth	*oya shirazu*	親不知(おやしらず)

At the Optometrist

contact lens	*kontakuto renzu*	コンタクト・レンズ
eye	*me*	目
eye drops	*me gusuri*	目薬
eye test	*shiryoku kensa*	視力検査
glasses	*megane*	眼鏡(めがね)
long-sighted	*en-shi*	遠視
optometrist	*shiryoku kentei shi*	視力検定師
pupil	*hitomi*	瞳(ひとみ)
short-sighted	*kin-gan*	近眼

Some Useful Words

accident	*jiko*	事故
acupuncture	*hari kyū*	針灸
acute	*kyūsei*	急性
AIDS	*eizu*	エイズ
antibiotic	*kōsei busshitsu*	抗生物質
antiseptic	*shōdoku*	消毒
bandage	*hōtai*	包帯
blood	*shukketsu*	出血
blood donation	*ken ketsu*	献血
blood pressure	*ketsu atsu*	血圧
blood group	*ketsu eki gata*	血液型
blood test	*ketsu eki kensa*	血液検査
cancer	*gan*	癌

HEALTH

Chinese medicine	*kampō yaku*	漢方薬
chronic	*man sei*	慢性
consulting room	*shinryō shitsu*	診療室
contraceptive	*piru*	ピル
dispensary	*yakkyoku*	薬局
doctor	*isha*	医者
first aid	*ōkyū teate*	応急手当
general practitioner	*kaigyōi*	開業医
high blood pressure	*kō ketsuatsu*	高血圧
history	*byōreki*	病歴
influenza	*infuruenza*	インフルエンザ
infrared rays	*sekigai sen*	赤外線
injection	*chūsha*	注射
low blood pressure	*tei ketsuatsu*	低血圧
meningitis	*nōmaku en*	脳膜炎
menstruation	*gekkei*	月経
nauseous	*hakike*	吐き気
No Visitors!	*menkai shazetsu*	面会謝絶
physiotherapist	*rigakuryōhō shi*	理学療法師
pneumonia	*hai en*	肺炎
pus	*umi*	膿(うみ)
recover	*naori masu*	治ります
Red Cross	*seki jūji*	赤十字
specialist	*semmon-i*	専門医
surgeon	*geka-i*	外科医
ultrasound	*chō ompa*	超音波
unconscious	*ishiki fumei*	意識不明
virus	*uirusu*	ウィルス
vitamin	*bitamin*	ビタミン
X-ray	*rentogen*	レントゲン

Times, Dates & Festivals

Telling the Time
Hours

To specify an hour, add the Chinese number (see the Numbers & Amounts chapter) to the word *-ji* 'o'clock':

three o'clock	*san-ji*	三時
five o'clock	*go-ji*	五時
Note:		
four o'clock	*yo-ji* (not *shi-ji*).	四時

• To say 'half past' use *-ji han*:

half past five	*go-ji han*	五時半

• To say 'It is' a certain time, follow the time with *desu*:

It's five o'clock.	*go-ji desu*	五時です

• To say 'at' a certain time, follow the time with *ni*:

(I came) at five o'clock.	*go-ji ni (kimashita)*	五時に（来ました）

Minutes

Combining numbers with minutes produces some special forms:

one minute	*ip-pun*	一分
two minutes	*ni-fun*	二分
three minutes	*sam-pun*	三分
four minutes	*yom-pun*	四分
five minutes	*go-fun*	五分
six minutes	*rop-pun*	六分
seven minutes	*shichi-fun/nana-fun*	七分
eight minutes	*hap-pun*	八分
nine minutes	*kyū-fun*	九分
10 minutes	*jip-pun*	十分
20 minutes	*ni-jip-pun*	二十分
5.20	*go-ji ni-jip-pun*	五時二十分

Time Of Day

If you want to specify morning or afternoon, say the appropriate word before the time:

in the morning	*gozen*	午前
	or *asa*	朝
noon	*hiru*	昼
in the afternoon	*gogo*	午後
in the evening	*yoru*	夜
10.00 am	*gozen jūji*	午前十時
2.30 pm	*gogo niji han*	午後二時半

Years

this year	*kotoshi*	ことし
last year	*kyonen*	去年
next year	*rainen*	来年

| one year | *ichi nen* | 一年 |
| two years | *ni nen* | 二年 |

Seasons

The rainy season begins in the middle of June and lasts for a month. It is sometimes called 'plum rain', *baiu*, as plum trees ripen at this time.

spring	*haru*	春
summer	*natsu*	夏
autumn	*aki*	秋
winter	*fuyu*	冬
seasons	*kisetsu*	季節
rainy season	*tsuyu/baiu*	梅雨

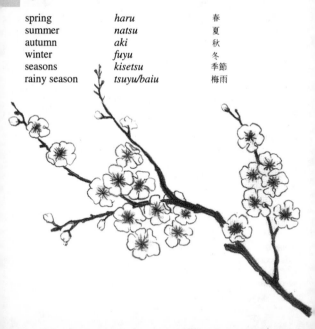

Months

Just add *gatsu* to the appropriate number:

January	*ichi gatsu*	一月
February	*ni gatsu*	二月
March	*san gatsu*	三月
April	*shi gatsu*	四月
May	*go gatsu*	五月
June	*roku gatsu*	六月
July	*shichi gatsu*	七月
August	*hachi gatsu*	八月
September	*ku gatsu*	九月
October	*jū gatsu*	十月
November	*jūichi gatsu*	十一月
December	*jūni gatsu*	十二月
Which month?	*nan gatsu desu ka?*	何月ですか？
this month	*kon getsu*	今月
last month	*sen getsu*	先月
next month	*rai getsu*	来月

Days

the day after tomorrow	*asatte*	あさって
the day before yesterday	*ototoi*	おととい
every day	*mai nichi*	毎日
festival	*o-matsuri*	お祭り
holiday	*kyū jitsu*	休日
this morning	*kesa*	今朝
today	*kyō*	今日

tomorrow	*asu*	明日
	or *ashita*	あした
yesterday	*kinō*	きのう

National Holidays

1 January	New Year	*ganjitsu*	元日
15 January	Adults' Day	*seijin no hi*	成人の日
11 February	National Foundation Day	*kenkoku kinen no hi*	建国記念の日
21 March	Vernal Equinox Day	*shumbun no hi*	春分の日
29 April	Green Day	*midori no hi*	緑の日
3 May	Constitution Day	*kempō kinem bi*	憲法記念日
5 May	Children's Day	*kodomo no hi*	子供の日
15 September	Respect for the Aged Day	*keirō no hi*	敬老の日
23 September	Autumnal Equinox Day	*shūbun no hi*	秋分の日
10 October	Sports Day	*taiiku no hi*	体育の日
3 November	Culture Day	*bunka no hi*	文化の日
23 November	Labour Thanks-giving Day	*kinrō kansha no hi*	勤労感謝の日
23 December	Emperor's Birthday	*tennō tanjōbi*	天皇誕生日

Traditional Festivals

Beginning of January	New Year	*o-shōgatsu*	お正月
3 May	Doll Festival	*hina matsuri*	雛祭り
April	Blossom Viewing	*o-hanami*	お花見
15 November	7-5-3 Birthday Ceremony	*shichi-go-san*	七五三
31 December	New Year's Eve	*ōmisoka*	大晦日

Chinese Festivals

5 May	Iris Festival	*tango no sekku*	端午の節句
7 July	Star Festival	*tanabata*	七夕
July or August	Buddhist All Souls' Day	*o-bon*	お盆
15 August	Moon Festival	*o-tsukimi* or *chūshū no meigetsu*	お月見 中秋の名月

Lucky & Unlucky Dates

Some Japanese still follow a traditional calendar which recognises certain times as auspicious or inauspicious for particular undertakings. There are six special days, or *rokuyō* (which will fall on different days each year of the Western Calendar): *taian* is an all-purpose lucky day, popular for weddings, moving house and travelling; *butsumetsu* and *shakkō* are unlucky days; *senshō* is lucky only in the morning; *sempu* means a period of good luck in the afternoon; and *tomobiki* signifies ill-fortune at noon. Funerals are also usually avoided on *tomobiki*.

rokuyō	六曜
butsumetsu	仏滅
sempu	先負
senshō	先勝
shakkō	赤口
taian	大安
tomobiki	友引

Western Festivals

14 February	Valentine's Day	*barentain dē*	バレンタイン・デー
14 March	White Day	*howaito dē*	ホワイト・デー
1 May	May Day	*mei dē*	メイ・デー
2nd Sunday of May	Mother's Day	*haha no hi*	母の日
3rd Sunday of June	Father's Day	*chichi no hi*	父の日
25 December	Christmas	*kurisumasu*	クリスマス

Days of the Week

Sunday	*nichi yōbi*	日曜日
Monday	*getsu yōbi*	月曜日
Tuesday	*ka yōbi*	火曜日
Wednesday	*sui yōbi*	水曜日
Thursday	*moku yōbi*	木曜日
Friday	*kin yōbi*	金曜日
Saturday	*do yōbi*	土曜日

Which day?	*nan yōbi desu ka?*	何曜日ですか？
this week	*kon shū*	今週
last week	*sen shū*	先週
next week	*rai shū*	来週

Some Useful Words

after	*... no ato*	...の後
always	*itsumo*	いつも
at the moment	*genzai*	現在
before	*... no mae ni*	...の前に
birthday	*tanjōbi*	誕生日
date of birth	*sei nen gappi*	生年月日
early	*hayai*	早い
evening	*yūgata*	夕方
future	*shōrai*	将来
late	*osoi*	遅い
night	*yoru*	夜
now	*ima*	今
recently	*saikin*	最近
soon	*sugu*	すぐ

Numbers & Amounts

Cardinal Numbers
Japanese has two sets of numbers, one being native Japanese and the other being of Chinese origin. Which one you use depends on what you are counting.

Japanese Numbers
The Japanese set only goes up to 10. These are used for counting objects.

1	*hitotsu*	一つ
2	*futatsu*	二つ
3	*mittsu*	三つ
4	*yottsu*	四つ
5	*itsutsu*	五つ
6	*muttsu*	六つ
7	*nanatsu*	七つ
8	*yattsu*	八つ
9	*kokonotsu*	九つ
10	*too*	十

Please give me (four).
   (yottsu) kudasai   （四つ）下さい

(Two) coffees, please.
   kōhī o (futatsu) kudasai   コーヒーを（二つ）下さい

(One) apple and (three) oranges, please.
   ringo o (hitotsu) to orenji o   リンゴを（一つ）と
   (mittsu) kudasai   オレンジを（三つ）下さい

Chinese Numbers

1	*ichi*	一
2	*ni*	二
3	*san*	三
4	*shi/yo/yon*	四
5	*go*	五
6	*roku*	六
7	*shichi/nana*	七
8	*hachi*	八
9	*ku/kyū*	九
10	*jū*	十

The numbers above 10 are easy to form: for example, 13 *jū san* is just a combination of the words for 10 *(jū)* and three *(san)*.

11	*jū ichi*	十一
12	*jū ni*	十二
13	*jū san*	十三
14	*jū shi/yo/yon*	十四
15	*jū go*	十五
16	*jū roku*	十六
17	*jū shichi/nana*	十七

18	*jū hachi*	十八
19	*jū kyū/ku*	十九
20	*ni jū*	二十
21	*ni jū ichi*	二十一
22	*ni jū ni*	二十二
28	*ni jū hachi*	二十八
30	*san jū*	三十
36	*san jū roku*	三十六
40	*yon jū*	四十
50	*go jū*	五十
60	*roku jū*	六十
70	*nana jū*	七十
80	*hachi jū*	八十
90	*kyū jū*	九十
99	*kyū jū kyū*	九十九
100	*hyaku*	百
113	*hyaku jū san*	百十三
200	*ni hyaku*	二百
999	*kyū hyaku kyū jū kyū*	九百九十九
1000	*sen*	千
1001	*sen ichi*	千一
1200	*sen ni hyaku*	千二百
3000	*san zen*	三千
10,000	*ichi man*	一万
100,000	*jū man*	十万
112,000	*jū ichi man ni sen*	十一万二千
1 million	*hyaku man*	百万
1,230,000	*hyaku ni jū sam man*	百二十三万
10 million	*issem man*	一千万
100 million	*ichi oku*	一億

Money

Chinese numbers are used with currencies such as *en* 'yen', *doru* 'dollar', *pondo* 'pound'. The numeral comes before the noun, as in English:

| ¥15,200 | *ichi-man go-sen ni-hyaku en* | 一万五千二百円 |
| $100 | *hyaku doru* | 100ドル |

How many?	*ikutsu desu ka?*	幾つですか?
How much?	*ikura desu ka?*	幾らですか?
enough	*jūbun*	十分
too expensive	*taka sugi masu*	高過ぎます
small change	*kozeni*	小銭
coin	*koin*	コイン
note	*satsu*	札(さつ)
a lot	*takusan*	沢山(たくさん)

How Many Times

The word *-kai* is added to a Chinese numeral to show 'how many times':

I've been to Yokohama (twice).

    Yokohama ni (ni-kai) iki-mashita 横浜に(2回)行きました

Telling the Time

Chinese numbers are also used for telling the time. See the Times, Dates & Festivals chapter.

Measure Words

Chinese numbers can also be used to count objects and people. However, to combine a Chinese number with a noun you have to use a 'measure word' (or 'counter'). The measure word you choose depends on what the object looks like. For example, *-mai* is used for thin flat objects such as tickets, sheets of paper and photographs:

one photo	*shashin ichi-mai*	写真一枚
	or *ichi-mai no shashin*	一枚の写真

Sometimes the first letter of a measure word changes depending on the numeral it follows: for example, the measure word for cups is usually *-hai*, but after one, six, eight and ten it becomes *-pai*, and after three it becomes *-bai*. In addition, the numeral itself sometimes changes in combination with a measure word: 'one cup' is ip-pai (not ichi-pai). However, if you use the normal Chinese numeral you will be understood.

Here is a list of the other most common measure words:

animals
  -tō   ... 頭(... とう)
books, magazines
  -satsu   ... 冊(... さつ)
bottles, pens, wire
  -pon after one/six/eight/ten   ... 本(... ぽん)
  -bon after three   ... 本(... ぼん)
  -hon after two/four/five/seven/nine   ... 本(... ほん)
buildings, shops
  -gen after three   ... 軒(... げん)
  -ken for others   ... 軒(... けん)
fish, some animals
  -piki after one/six/eight/ten   ... 匹(... ぴき)

-biki after three		...匹(...びき)
-hiki after two/four/five/seven/nine		...匹(...ひき)
floor		
-gai after three		...階(...がい)
-kai for others		...階(...かい)
letters, telephones		
-tsū		...通(...つう)
pieces		
-ko		...個(...こ)
shoes, socks		
-zoku after three		...足(...ぞく)
-soku for others		...足(...そく)
vehicles		
-dai		...台(...だい)

NUMBERS

Measurement

Japan officially uses the metric system.

km	*kiro*	キロ
metre	*mētoru*	メートル
centimetre	*senchi*	センチ
millimetre	*miri*	ミリ

My height is (182) cm.
    shin chō (ichi mētoru hachi-jūni) 身長(1メートル82) センチ
    senchi

kg	*kiro guramu/kiro*	キログラム/キロ
gram	*guramu*	グラム
200 grams	*ni-hyaku guramu*	200グラム
litre	*rittoru*	リットル

Please give me two kilos (of ...)
(... o) ni kiro kudasai   （．．．を）2キロ下さい

Japanese also has some traditional words for measurement such as *jō* (about 180cm x 90cm), literally 'straw mat', to measure the size of a room; and *tsubo* (about 3.3 m^2) to measure land or floorspace:

a four-and-a-half 'mat' room
yo jō han no heya   4畳半の部屋
a one hundred *tsubo* hall
hyaku tsubo no hōru   100坪のホール

Percentages & Decimals
Use the borrowed word *pāsento* after the Chinese number:

15%   *jū go pāsento*   15パーセント

This is useful when shopping for bargains:

15% off   *jū go pāsento biki*   15パーセント引き

Ordinal Numbers
To say 'first, second, third ...' just add *ban* to the Chinese number:

1st   *ichi ban*   一番
2nd   *ni ban*   二番
5th   *go ban*   五番

Some Useful Words

about	*yaku*	約
amount	*kin gaku*	金額
calculate	*keisan shi masu*	計算します
count	*kazoe masu*	数えます
(A) divided by (B)	*(A) waru (B)*	(A)割る(B)
double	*ni bai*	二倍
a dozen	*ichi dāsu*	1ダース
few	*sukoshi*	少し
first time	*hajimete*	初めて
half	*ham-bun*	半分
half price	*han gaku*	半額
Japanese Yen	*nihon en*	日本円
last	*saigo*	最後
	or *ichi ban saigo*	一番最後
less	*sukunai*	少ない
(A) minus (B)	*(A) hiku (B)*	(A)引く(B)
more	*motto*	もっと
number	*sūji*	数字
once	*ikkai*	一回
a pair	*pea*	ペア
(A) plus (B)	*(A) tasu (B)*	(A)足す(B)
(A) times (B)	*(A) kakeru (B)*	(A)掛ける(B)
total (amount)	*gōkei (kingaku)*	合計(金額)
triple	*sam-bai*	3倍
twice	*ni-kai*	2回

Vocabulary

A

about – *yaku*	約	
above – *no ue ni*	…の上に	
accident – *jiko*	事故	
acquaintance – *shiriai*	知合い	
adult – *otona*	大人	
address – *jūsho*	住所	
agency – *dairi ten*	代理店	
agree (v) – *dōi shimasu*	同意します	
AIDS – *eizu*	エイズ	
airport – *kū kō*	空港	
already – *sudeni*	既に	
also – *mata*	また	
always – *itsumo*	いつも	
angry – *okori masu*	怒ります	
animal – *dōbutsu*	動物	
answer – *kotae*	答え	
anything – *nan demo*	何でも	
any time – *itsu demo*	いつでも	
anywhere – *doko demo*	どこでも	
arm – *ude*	腕	
art gallery – *bijutsu kan*	美術館	
artist – *geijutsu ka*	芸術家	
ashamed – *hazukashii*	恥ずかしい	
ashtray – *hai zara*	灰皿	
ask (v) – *kiki masu*	聞きます	
asleep – *nemutte imasu*	眠っています	

B

baby food – *rinyū shoku* 離乳食
baby powder – *bebī paudā* ベビー・パウダー
back – *senaka* 背中
bag – *baggu* バッグ
baggage – *tenimotsu* 手荷物
bank – *ginkō* 銀行
banquet – *enkai* 宴会
bargain – *bāgen* バーゲン
Bible – *seisho* 聖書
big – *ookii* 大きい
bill – *kanjōsho* 勘定書
bird – *tori* 鳥
bitter – *nigai* 苦い
black – *kuro* 黒
blanket – *mōfu* 毛布
book (v) – *yoyaku shimasu* 予約します
book – *hon* 本
booking – *yoyaku* 予約
bookshop – *hon ya* 本屋
botanic garden – *shokubutsu kōen* 植物公園
bridge – *hashi* 橋
bright – *akarui* 明るい
broken – *kowareta* 壊れた
building – *tatemono* 建物
bullet train – *shinkansen* 新幹線
bus – *basu* バス
bus stop – *basu tei* バス停
bus terminal – *basu tāminaru* バス・ターミナル
businessman – *bijinesu man* ビジネス・マン
businesswoman – *bijinesu ūman* ビジネス・ウーマン

busy – *isogashii* 忙しい
button – *botan* ボタン
buy (v) – *kai masu* 買います

C

camera – *kamera* カメラ
cancel – *torikeshi* 取消し
car – *kuruma* 車
car park – *chūshajō* 駐車場
cash – *genkin* 現金
castle – *shiro* 城
casual dress – *kajuaru doresu* カジュアル・ドレス
cat – *neko* 猫
chair – *isu* 椅子
change over – *norikae* 乗換え
cheap – *yasui* 安い
checkers – *go* 碁
cheque – *kogitte* 小切手
cherry blossom – *sakura* 桜
chinaware – *setomono* 瀬戸物
Chinese food – *chūka ryōri* 中華料理
Chinese tea – *chūgoku cha* 中国茶
chocolate – *chokorēto* チョコレート
Christmas card – *kurisumasu kādo* クリスマス・カード
chrysanthemum – *kiku* 菊
church – *kyōkai* 教会
cigarette – *tabako* たばこ
cinema – *eiga kan* 映画館
circus – *sākasu* サーカス
classical music – *kurashikku* クラシック
clean – *seiketsu na* 清潔な...

clock – *tokei* 時計
clothing – *irui* 衣類
coffee – *kōhī* コーヒー
coins – *koin* コイン
cold – *tsumetai* 冷たい
cold (weather) – *samui* 寒い
cold water – *o-mizu* お水
comic – *manga* 漫画
company – *kaisha* 会社
concert – *konsāto* コンサート
condom – *kondōmu* コンドーム
consulate – *ryōji kan* 領事館
contraceptive – *hininyaku* 避妊薬
corner – *kado* 角
cosmetics – *keshōhin* 化粧品
count (v) – *kazoe masu* 数えます
counter – *kauntā* カウンター
country – *kuni* 国
countryside – *inaka* 田舎
crab – *kani* 蟹(カニ)
crane – *tsuru* 鶴
cupboard – *oshiire* 押入れ
cushions – *zabuton* 座布団
cuttlefish – *ika* 烏賊(イカ)

D

dance – *dansu* ダンス
Danger! – *abunai!* 危ない！
dark – *kurai* 暗い
delicious – *oishii* 美味しい
desert – *sabaku* 砂漠

dialect – *hōgen* 方言
dictionary – *jisho* 辞書
different – *kotonaru* 異なる
difficult – *muzukashii* 難しい
direction – *hōkō* 方向
directory – *denwa chō* 電話帳
dirty – *kitanai* 汚い
disco – *disuko* ディスコ
discount – *waribiki* 割引
divorced – *rikon* 離婚
doctor – *isha* 医者
dog – *inu* 犬
doll (Japanese) – *ningyō* 人形
double – *ni bai* 二倍
driver – *unten shu* 運転手
drivers' licence – *unten menkyo* 運転免許
drugs – *kusuri* 薬

E

ear – *mimi* 耳
early – *hayai* 早い
earn (v) – *kasegi masu* 稼ぎます
earthquake – *jishin* 地震
easy – *yasashii* 易しい
eat (v) – *tabe masu* 食べます
editor – *henshūsha* 編集者
egg – *tamago* 玉子
elbow – *hiji* 肘
electricity – *denki* 電気
embassy – *taishi kan* 大使館
emergency exit – *hijyō guchi* 非常口

entrance – *iri guchi* 入り口
envelope – *fūtō* 封筒
exchange rate – *kawase rēto* 為替レート
exit – *de guchi* 出口
expensive – *takai* 高い
express mail – *sokutatsu* 速達
eye – *me* 目
eye drops – *me gusuri* 目薬

F

face – *kao* 顔
fall (v) – *ochi masu* 落ちます
fan (folding) – *sensu* 扇子
fan (round) – *uchiwa* 団扇
far away – *tooi* 遠い
fast – *hayai* 速い
favourite – *konomi* 好み
fax – *fakkusu* ファックス
fee – *ryōkin* 料金
few – *sukoshi* 少し
fight – *kenka* 喧嘩
film – *firumu* フィルム
finish (v) – *owari masu* 終わります
fire extinguisher – *shōka ki* 消火器
fire – *kaji* 火事
first time – *hajimete* はじめて
first aid kit – *kyūkyūbako* 救急箱
fish – *sakana* 魚
flash – *furasshu* フラッシュ
flood – *kōzui* 洪水
florist – *hana ya* 花屋

flower arrangement – *ike bana*	生け花
flower – *hana*	花
fly – *hae*	蝿
folding screen – *byōbu*	屏風
foreign currency – *gaika*	外貨
foreign country – *gai-koku*	外国
foreign language – *gaikoku-go*	外国語
foreigner – *gai jin*	外人
fork – *fōku*	フォーク
freeway – *kōsoku dōro*	高速道路
friend – *o-tomodachi*	お友達
from – ... *kara*	...から
fruit shop – *kudamono ya*	果物屋
future – *shōrai*	将来

G

game – *gēmu*	ゲーム
get (v) – *te ni iremasu*	手に入れます
get off (v) – *ori masu*	降ります
get on (v) – *nori masu*	乗ります
geyser – *kanketsu sen*	間けつ泉
gift – *okuri mono*	贈り物
give (v) – *atae masu*	与えます
glass – *gurasu*	グラス
glasses – *megane*	眼鏡(メガネ)
go (v) – *iki masu*	行きます
God – *kami sama*	神様
good – *yoi*	よい
goods – *shina mono*	品物
grapefruit – *gurēpu furūtsu*	グレープ・フルーツ
grass – *kusa*	草

grassy plains – *sōgen*　　　　　　　草原
guest – *okyaku sama*　　　　　　　お客様

H

hair – *kaminoke*　　　　　　　　　髪の毛
half – *ham-bun*　　　　　　　　　　半分
half-price – *han gaku*　　　　　　　半額
handbag – *hando baggu*　　　　　　ハンド・バッグ
handmade – *te zukuri*　　　　　　　手作り
happy – *ureshii*　　　　　　　　　　嬉しい
hard, solid – *katai*　　　　　　　　堅い
hat – *bōshi*　　　　　　　　　　　　帽子
head – *atama*　　　　　　　　　　　頭
health food – *kenkō shoku*　　　　　健康食
heating – *dambō*　　　　　　　　　暖房
helmet (Japanese) – *kabuto*　　　　兜
Help! – *tasukete!*　　　　　　　　　助けて！
home – *ie*　　　　　　　　　　　　家
honey – *hachimitsu*　　　　　　　　蜂蜜
horseradish – *wasabi*　　　　　　　わさび
hospital – *byōin*　　　　　　　　　病院
hot (spicy) – *karai*　　　　　　　　辛い
hot (weather) – *atsui*　　　　　　　暑い
hot Japanese wine – *atsu kan*　　　熱燗
hot spring – *onsen*　　　　　　　　温泉
hot water – *o-yu*　　　　　　　　　お湯
hotel – *hoteru*　　　　　　　　　　ホテル

I

ice water – *o-hiya*　　　　　　　　お冷や
identification card – *mibun shōmei sho* 身分証明書

immediately – *sugu* すぐ
important – *jūyō* 重要
in front of – *... no mae ni* ...の前に
included – *... komi* ...込み
ingredient – *zairyō* 材料
inn – *ryokan* 旅館
inside – *... no naka ni* ...の中に
insurance – *hoken* 保険
international call – *kokusai denwa* 国際電話
interpreter – *tsūyaku* 通訳
iron – *airon* アイロン
island – *shima* 島

J

Japan – *nihon* 日本
Japanese food – *nihon shoku* 日本食
Japanese garden – *nihon teien* 日本庭園
jelly – *zerī* ゼリー
job – *shigoto* 仕事
journalist – *kisha* 記者
juice – *jūsu* ジュース
junction – *kōsaten* 交差点

K

karaoke – *kara oke* カラオケ
kelp – *kombu* 昆布
key – *kagi* 鍵
kiosk – *bai ten* 売店
kitchen (house) – *dai dokoro* 台所
kitchen (restaurant) – *chōri ba* 調理場
know (v) – *wakari masu* 分かります

L

lacquerware – *shikki* 漆器
lake – *mizuumi* 湖
language – *kotoba* 言葉
last – saigo 最後
lawn – *shibafu* 芝生
leaf – *ha* 葉
learn (v) – *manabi masu* 学びます
left – *hidari* 左
less – *sukunai* 少ない
letter – *tegami* 手紙
lettuce – *retasu* レタス
lily – *yuri* 百合(ユリ)
local call – *shinai denwa* 市内電話
lonely – *sabishii* 寂しい
long-distance call – *chōkyori denwa* 長距離電話
look (v) – *mi masu* 見ます
lookout – *miharashi dai* 見晴台
lounge – *raunji* ラウンジ
love – *ai* 愛
love (v) – *ai shimasu* 愛します
lovely – *kawaii* 可愛い
luggage – *nimotsu* 荷物
lunch box – *o-bentō* お弁当

M

magazine – *zasshi* 雑誌
magic show – *kijutsu* 奇術
mahjong – *mājan* マージャン
make (v) – *tsukuri masu* 作ります
manager – *manējā* マネージャー

map – *chizu*　　　　　　　　地図
market – *ichiba*　　　　　　　市場
mattress – *shiki buton*　　　　敷布団
menu – *me nyū*　　　　　　　メニュー
message – *messēji*　　　　　　メッセージ
middle, in the – *man naka*　　真ん中
milk – *miruku*　　　　　　　ミルク
mineral water – *mineraru uōtā*　ミネラル・ウォーター
mini bar – *mini bā*　　　　　ミニ・バー
mint – *hakka*　　　　　　　　薄荷
mirror – *kagami*　　　　　　鏡
mobile phone – *mōbiru denwa*　モービル電話
model – *moderu*　　　　　　　モデル
Monday – *getsu yōbi*　　　　月曜日
money – *okane*　　　　　　　お金
monorail – *monorēru*　　　　モノレール
more – *motto*　　　　　　　　もっと
Mosque – *mosuku*　　　　　　モスク
mountain – *yama*　　　　　　山
movie – *eiga*　　　　　　　　映画
MSG – *aji no moto*　　　　　味の素
museum – *hakubutsu kan*　　博物館
music – *ongaku*　　　　　　音楽
musical instrument – *gakki*　楽器
musician – *ongaku ka*　　　音楽家

N

nail clippers – *tsume kiri*　　爪切り
name – *namae*　　　　　　　名前
national park – *kokuritsu kōen*　国立公園

nationality – *kokuseki* 国籍
newspaper – *shimbun* 新聞
newspaper in English – *eigo no shimbun* 英語の新聞
next to – ... *no tonari* ...の隣り
nightclub – *kurabu* クラブ
noisy – *urusai* 煩い
nose – *hana* 鼻
now – *ima* 今
nurse (m) – *kangoshi* 看護士
nurse (f) – *kangofu* 看護婦

O

occupation – *shokugyō* 職業
ocean – *kaiyō* 海洋
office worker – *jimuin* 事務員
often – *yoku* よく
oil – *abura* 油
old – *furui* 古い
old person – *toshi yori* 年寄り
on sale – *yasu uri* 安売り
open (v) – *hiraki masu* 開きます
opera – *opera* オペラ
operator – *kōkanshu* 交換手
opposite side – *mamukai* 真向かい
or – *matawa* 又は
order – *chūmon* 注文
ordinary – *futsū* 普通
out of order – *koshō* 故障
out of stock – *shina gire* 品切れ
outside – *soto* 外

P

painting (Japanese) – *nihon ga* 日本画
paper (Japanese) – *washi* 和紙
parents – *ryōshin* 両親
park – *kōen* 公園
pass – *tōge* 峠
passport – *pasupōto* パスポート
pattern – *gara* 柄
pay (v) – *harai masu* 払います
peak – *mine* 峰
pearl – *shinju* 真珠
peninsula – *hantō* 半島
people – *hito* 人
personal seal – *inkan* 印鑑
petrol – *gasorin* ガソリン
petrol station – *gasorin sutando* ガソリン・スタンド
pharmacy – *yakkyoku* 薬局
photo – *shashin* 写真
picnic – *pikunikku* ピクニック
pill, the – *piru* ピル
pillow – *makura* 枕
police – *porisu* ポリス
police box – *kōban* 交番
poor – *mazushii* 貧しい
popular music – *popyurā myūjikku* ポピュラー・ミュージック
porter – *pōtā* ポーター
postcard – *hagaki* 葉書き
postcode – *yūbin bangō* 郵便番号
post office – *yūbin kyoku* 郵便局
pretty – *utsukushii* 美しい

price – *nedan* 値段
price tag – *nefuda* 値札
print – *purinto* プリント
printed matter – *insatsu butsu* 印刷物
program – *puroguramu* プログラム
public phone – *kōshū denwa* 公衆電話

Q

question – *shitsumon* 質問
queue – *gyōretsu* 行列
quickly – *subayaku* 素早く

R

radio – *rajio* ラジオ
rail crossing – *fumi kiri* 踏切り
rain – *ame* 雨
rainbow – *niji* 虹
rainy season – *tsuyu* 梅雨
razor – *kamisori* カミソリ
rear – *ushiro* 後ろ
receipt – *ryōshūsho* 領収書
receptionist – *uketsuke kakari* 受付係り
refund – *harai modoshi* 払戻し
register – *reji* レジ
relative – *shinseki* 親戚
religion – *shūkyō* 宗教
remember (v) – *oboe masu* 覚えます
rent (v) – *kari masu* 借ります
rent-a-car – *renta kā* レンター・カー
replacement – *dainōhin* 代納品
restaurant – *resutoran* レストラン

retired – *taishoku* 退職
return ticket – *ōfuku jōsha ken* 往復乗車券
rich – *kane mochi* 金持ち
right – *migi* 右
ring – *wa* 輪
ripe – *jukushita* 熟した
river – *kawa* 川
roadworks – *kōji chū* 工事中
room – *heya* 部屋
rope – *nawa* 縄
ruins – *iseki* 遺跡

S

sad – *kanashii* 悲しい
safe – *anzen* 安全
same – *onaji* 同じ
sandals (Japanese) – *zōri* 草履
sanitary napkins – *seiri yō napukin* 生理用ナプキン
sauna – *sauna* サウナ
scared – *kowai* 恐い
school – *gakkō* 学校
sculpture – *chōkoku* 彫刻
season – *kisetsu* 季節
secretary – *hisho* 秘書
sell (v) – *uri masu* 売ります
separated – *bekkyo* 別居
service charge – *sābisu ryō* サービス料
sew (v) – *nui masu* 縫います
shame – *hazukashii* 恥ずかしい
sheet – *shītsu* シーツ
shop – *mise* 店

shopping – *kaimono*	買い物
short-sighted – *kin-gan*	近眼
shorts – *han zubon*	半ズボン
shoulder – *kata*	肩
show – *shō*	ショー
shower – *shawā*	シャワー
shrine – *jinja*	神社
sightseeing – *kankō*	観光
signature – *sain*	サイン
silkworm – *kaiko*	蚕
singing – *uta*	唄
size – *saizu*	サイズ
skin – *hifu*	皮膚
sky – *sora*	空
sleep (v) – *nemuri masu*	眠ります
sleeping bag – *surīpingu baggu*	スリーピング・バッグ
sleeping pill – *suimin yaku*	睡眠薬
sleepy – *nemui*	眠い
slippers – *surippa*	スリッパ
slow – *jokō*	徐行
small – *chiisai*	小さい
small change – *kozeni*	小銭
snow – *yuki*	雪
soccer – *sakkā*	サッカー
socks – *kutsushita*	靴下
soldier – *gun jin*	軍人
soon – *sugu*	すぐ
sour – *suppai*	酸っぱい
souvenir shop – *miyage mono ya*	土産物屋
soy sauce – *shōyu*	醤油
spectacles – *megane*	眼鏡

spicy – *karai* 　　　　　　　辛い
stamps – *kitte* 　　　　　　　切手
star – *hoshi* 　　　　　　　　星
station – *eki* 　　　　　　　　駅
statue – *dōzō* 　　　　　　　　銅像
steal (v) – *nusumi masu* 　　　盗みます
strange – *okashii* 　　　　　　おかしい
strong – *tsuyoi* 　　　　　　　強い
student discount – *gaku wari* 　学割
student – *gakusei* 　　　　　　学生
subway station – *chikatetsu eki* 地下鉄駅
subway – *chikatetsu* 　　　　　地下鉄
supermarket – *sūpā māketto* 　スーパー・マーケット
supper – *yashoku* 　　　　　　夜食
surfing – *sāfin* 　　　　　　　サーフィン
swan – *haku chō* 　　　　　　　白鳥
sweat – *ase* 　　　　　　　　　汗
sweet – *amai* 　　　　　　　　甘い
swim (v) – *oyogi masu* 　　　　泳ぎます
sword – *katana* 　　　　　　　刀

T

table – *tsukue* 　　　　　　　　机
tag – *taggu* 　　　　　　　　　タッグ
taxi – *takushī* 　　　　　　　　タクシー
tea (Japanese) – *o-cha* 　　　　お茶
tea (Western) – *kōcha* 　　　　紅茶
tea ceremony – *sadō* 　　　　　茶道
teacher – *kyōshi* 　　　　　　　教師
teapot – *kyūsu* 　　　　　　　　急須
teeth – *ha* 　　　　　　　　　　歯

telegram – *dempō* 電報
telephone – *denwa* 電話
telephone booth – *denwa bokkusu* 電話ボックス
telephone card – *terehon kādo* テレホン・カード
telephone charge – *denwa ryōkin* 電話料金
telephone number – *denwa bangō* 電話番号
telephone operator – *kōkan shu* 交換手
television – *terebi* テレビ
temple – *o-tera* お寺
terminal – *tāminaru* ターミナル
theft – *tōnan* 盗難
thermometer – *taion kei* 体温計
thief – *dorobō* 泥棒
thirsty – *kawaki* 渇き
thunder – *kaminari* 雷
ticket – *kippu* 切符
tiger – *tora* 虎
tiger balm – *taigā bāmu* タイガー・バーム
timetable – *jikokuhyō* 時刻表
tip (money) – *chippu* チップ
today – *kyō* 今日
together with – *... to issho ni* …と一緒に
toilet paper – *toiretto pēpā* トイレット・ペーパー
toilet – *o-tearai* お手洗い
tomorrow – *asu* 明日
total (amount) – *gōkei (kingaku)* 合計（金額）
tour guide – *tenjō in* 添乗員
tourist – *kankō kyaku* 観光客
towel – *taoru* タオル
traffic light – *shingō* 信号
train – *densha* 電車

travel sickness pill – *yoi dome*   酔止め
travellers' cheque – *ryokō kogitte*   旅行小切手
tree – *ki*   木
trousers – *zubon*   ズボン
TV – *terebi*   テレビ

U

ugly – *minikui*   醜い
umbrella – *kasa*   傘
understand (v) – *wakari masu*   分かります
universe – *uchū*   宇宙
university – *dai gaku*   大学
upstairs – *ue*   上
useful – *yūyō teki na*   有用的な

V

vaccination – *yobō chūsha*   予防注射
valley – *tani*   谷
vegetarian food – *yasai ryōri*   野菜料理
vending machine – *jidō hambaiki*   自動販売機
very – *totemo*   とても
via – ... *keiyu*   ...経由
village – *mura*   村
virus – *uirusu*   ウィルス
visa – *biza*   ビザ
voltage – *den atsu*   電圧

W

wait (v) – *machi masu*   待ちます
waiting room – *machiai shitsu*   待合室
walk (v) – *aruki masu*   歩きます

wallet – *saifu* 財布
warm up (v) – *atatame masu* 暖めます
watch – *ude dokei* 腕時計
water – *mizu* 水
waterfall – *taki* 滝
weak – *yowai* 弱い
weigh (v) – *hakari masu* 計ります
well – *yoi* よい
Western food – *seiyō ryōri* 西洋料理
wet – *nure* 濡れ
wind – *kaze* 風
window – *mado* 窓
window seat – *mado gawa* 窓側の席
　　　　　no seki
wine list – *wain risuto* ワイン・リスト
wine glass – *wain gurasu* ワイン・グラス
wine (Japanese) – *sake* 酒
wonderful – *subarashii* 素晴らしい
woodblock print (Japanese) – *ukiyo-e* 浮世絵
word processor – *wāpuro* ワープロ
work (v) – *hataraki masu* 働きます
worry – *shimpai* 心配
write (v) – *kaki masu* 書きます
writer – *sakka* 作家
wrong number – *machigai denwa* 間違い電話

Y

yacht – *yotto* ヨット
yellowtail – *aji* 鰺
yen – *en* 円
yesterday – *kinō* きのう

youth hostel – *yūsu hosuteru*　　　ユース・ホステル

Z
zoo – *dōbutsu en*　　　　　　　　動物園

Emergencies

Danger!	*abunai!*	危ない！
	or *kiken!*	危険！
Earthquake!	*jishin!*	地震
Fire!	*kaji!*	火事
Help!	*tasukete!*	助けて！
Stop!	*tomare!*	止れ！
Thief!	*dorobō!*	泥棒！

Reporting an Emergency

There has been an accident.
   asoko de jiko ga ari mashita   あそこで事故が ありました

There has been a collision.
   asoko de shōtotsu jiko ga   あそこで衝突事故がありました
   ari mashita

There is a fight.
   asoko de kenka shite i masu   あそこで喧嘩して います

Someone has been injured.
   kega o shite iru hito ga i masu   怪我をしている人が います

I have been injured.
   watashi wa kega shi mashita   私は怪我しました

I have been raped.
   watashi wa reipu sare mashita   私はレイプされました

I have been robbed.
   dorobō ni hairare mashita   泥棒に入られました

I have lost my ...	... o naku shi mashita	...をなくしました
Someone's taken my ...	... o torare mashita	...を取られました
backpack	bakku pakku	バック・パック
bag	baggu	バッグ
camera	kamera	カメラ
handbag	hando baggu	ハンド・バッグ
luggage	nimotsu	荷物
money	o-kane	お金
passport	pasupōto	パスポート
ticket	kippu	切符
wallet	saifu	財布
watch	ude dokei	腕時計

Call ...	... o yonde kudasai	...を呼んで下さい
an ambulance	kyūkyūsha	救急車
a doctor	isha	医者
the fire brigade	shōbōsho	消防署
a fire engine	shōbōsha	消防車
the police	keisatsu	警察

Getting Medical Attention

He/She needs a doctor.

    o-isha ni kakaru hitsuyō ga ari masu   お医者にかかる必要があります

He/She needs first aid.

    ōkyūteate ga hitsuyō desu   応急手当が必要です

He/She needs to go to a hospital.

    byōin ni ikanakute wa nari masen   病院に行かなくては なりません

He/She needs mouth-to-mouth resuscitation.

(kare)/(kanojo) wa jinkō kokyū shinakereba nari masen

(彼)/(彼女)は人工呼吸しなければなりません

What is (your) blood type?

(anata no) ketsueki gata wa nan desu ka?

(あなたの)血液型は何ですか？

My blood type is A/B/O/AB Positive/Negative.

watashi no ketsueki gata wa (A/B/O/AB) (purasu)/(mainasu) desu

私の血液型は（A / B / O / AB）（プラス）/（マイナス）です

Please don't move.

ugokanaide kudasai

動かないで下さい

Some Useful Phrases

Where is the toilet?

o-tearai wa dochira desu ka?

お手洗いはどちらですか？

I am lost.

watashi wa mayoi mashita

私は迷いました

I wish to contact my ...

... ni renraku shitai desu

...に連絡したいです

company	*kaisha*	会社
consulate	*ryōji kan*	領事館
embassy	*taishi kan*	大使館
home	*jitaku*	自宅
lawyer	*bengoshi*	弁護士

EMERGENCIES

Index

Language Survival Kits

Complete your travel experience with a Lonely Planet phrasebook. Developed for the independent traveller, the phrasebooks enable you to communicate confidently in any practical situation – and get to know the local people and their culture.

Skipping lengthy details on where to get your drycleaning ironed, information in the phrasebooks covers bargaining, customs and protocol, how to address people and introduce yourself, explanations of local ways of telling the time, dealing with bureaucracy and bargaining, plus plenty of ways to share your interests and learn from locals.

Australian
Introduction to Australian English, Aboriginal and Torres Strait languages.
Arabic (Egyptian)
Arabic (Moroccan)
Baltic States
Covers Estonian, Latvian and Lithuanian.
Brazilian
Burmese
Cantonese
Central Europe
Covers Czech, French, German, Hungarian, Italian and Slovak.
Eastern Europe
Covers Bulgarian, Czech, Hungarian, Polish, Romanian and Slovak.
Fijian
Greek
Hindi/Urdu
Indonesian
Japanese
Korean
Lao
Mandarin
Mediterranean Europe
Covers Albanian, Greek, Italian, Macedonian, Maltese, Serbian & Croatian and Slovene.

Mongolian
Nepali
Papua New Guinea
Pilipino
Quechua
Russian
Scandinavian Europe
Covers Danish, Finnish, Icelandic, Norwegian and Swedish.
Spanish (Latin American)
Sri Lanka
Swahili
Thai
Thai Hill Tribes
Tibet
Turkish
USA
Introduction to US English, Vernacular Talk, Native American languages and Hawaiian.
Vietnamese
Western Europe
Useful words and phrases in Basque, Catalan, Dutch, French, German, Irish, Portuguese and Spanish (Castilian).

Lonely Planet Audio Packs

The best way to learn a language is to hear it spoken in context. Set within a dramatic narrative, with local music and local speakers, is a wide range of words and phrases for the independent traveller – to help you talk to people you meet, make your way around more easily, and enjoy your stay.

Each pack includes a phrasebook and CD or cassette, and comes in an attractive, useful cloth bag. These bags are made by local community groups, using traditional methods.

Forthcoming Language Survival Kits
Bengali, Sinhalese, Hebrew, Ukrainian, Ethiopian (Amharic)

Forthcoming Audio Packs
Indonesian, Japanese, Thai, Vietnamese, Mandarin, Cantonese

PLANET TALK

Lonely Planet's FREE quarterly newsletter

We love hearing from you and think you'd
like to hear from us.

*When...is the right time to see reindeer in
Finland?*
*Where...can you hear the best palm-wine music in
Ghana?*
*How...do you get from Asunción to Areguá by
steam train?*
*What...should you leave behind to avoid hassles
with customs in Iran?*

For the answer to these and many other questions read PLANET TALK.

Every issue is packed with up-to-date travel news and advice including:

- *a letter from Lonely Planet founders Tony and Maureen Wheeler*
- *travel diary from a Lonely Planet author - find out what it's really like out
  on the road*
- *feature article on an important and topical travel issue*
- *a selection of recent letters from our readers*
- *the latest travel news from all over the world*
- *details on Lonely Planet's new and forthcoming releases*

To join our mailing list contact any Lonely Planet office.

LONELY PLANET PUBLICATIONS
Australia: PO Box 617, Hawthorn 3122, Victoria
tel: (03) 9819 1877 fax: (03) 9819 6459 e-mail: talk2us@lonelyplanet.com.au

USA: Embarcadero West, 155 Filbert St, Suite 251, Oakland, CA 94607
tel: (510) 893 8555 TOLL FREE: 800 275-8555 fax: (510) 893 8563
e-mail: info@lonelyplanet.com

UK: 10 Barley Mow Passage, Chiswick, London W4 4PH
tel: (0181) 742 3161 fax: (0181) 742 2772 e-mail: 100413.3551@compuserve.com

France: 71 bis rue du Cardinal Lemoine – 75005 Paris
tel: 1 46 34 00 58 fax: 1 46 34 72 55 e-mail: 100560.415@compuserve.com

World Wide Web: http://www.lonelyplanet.com/